Gospel-Telling

The Art And Theology
Of Children's Sermons

Richard J. Coleman

CSS Publishing Company, Inc., Lima, Ohio

GOSPEL-TELLING

Copyright © 2002 by
CSS Publishing Company, Inc.
Lima, Ohio

Library of Congress Cataloging-in-Publication Data

Coleman, Richard J.
  Gospel telling : the art and theology of children's sermons / Richard J. Coleman.
    p. cm.
Includes bibliographical references (p.   ).
  ISBN 0-7880-1949-X
  1. Preaching to children. 2. Children's sermons. 3. Sermons, American. I. Title.
BV4235.C4 C64 2003
251'.53—dc21

                              2002013717

For more information about CSS Publishing Company resources, visit our website at www.csspub.com or e-mail us at custserv@csspub.com or call (800) 241-4056.

ISBN 0-7880-1949-X   PRINTED IN U.S.A.

Dedicated to
my own three children:
Joy, Sharon, and Laura
and all the children
who have blessed my life
by simply being children

Table Of Contents

Part II — Variety: The Spice Of Gospel-Telling

Preface

In this handbook my purpose is *not* to provide the minister or religious educator with the usual 40 to 52 object lessons or children's sermons. My goal is to help the proclaimer create his or her own gospel stories by sensitizing him or her to what constitutes a good children's sermon and by illustrating the methodology outlined here with a variety of sermons. The ideas and development of sermons are always more appropriate and effective if they flow from the minister in his/her own particular situation. If this handbook succeeds, it will do so not because of any great originality on my part but because I have managed to impart my belief that within each of us is an unlimited source of creative ideas that can be developed into meaningful gospel messages for children. And I have taken the time to examine critically and theologically the method and content of what I do when proclaiming the love of God in Jesus Christ.

When we hear a good sermon, regardless of our age, we know it. We do not, however, usually know why, and as preachers we do not know how to repeat the experience. This should not stop us from thinking long and hard about our methodology, our theology, and our communication skills. Alas, if only we the proclaimers would care as much how the gospel is being proclaimed to children. Since the first publication of this book in 1982, I am pleased to report the enthusiasm for inclusive worship has intensified. The presence of children in worship is no longer viewed as a concession or as something we should merely tolerate. I hope we have moved beyond the cliché that they are the future of the church. Children join us for worship because the congregation is incomplete without them. They are as much the part of the church family as they are of any family. They are present because they need to learn how to worship and to lift up their voices in worship. They sit beside us and come to the front of the sanctuary to participate (not just hear) in the gospel, because corporate worship is a unique setting and a particular experience. Thus, we can rejoice in the about-face concerning our acceptance of children in worship but lament that we have been lax and careless in our preparation. This handbook is intended to prick the conscience of those who know they have paid insufficient attention to the way they communicate the gospel to children. How often have we waited until the last minute and then hurriedly paged through a book or racked our brains for a suitable nugget to offer our little ones? We can do better!

Doing better and doing it differently is what this book is about. I confess that the initial impulse to write this handbook came from a book of object lessons that turned me off. The more I thought about it, the more I was convinced I could do better. Thus the exploration began. As I became critical about object lessons I became critical about everything I was doing and took a "hard" look at everything that was happening when the children would join me on the chancel steps. It soon became clear that it was intolerable to tell children cute moralistic stories, simply to retell biblical stories, to read to them from a storybook, or to preach adult sermons reduced to a child's level. The gospel is more than good behavior and cannot be communicated to children by the same means as adult sermons. I would resist the temptation to substitute good behavior for the Good News and face the fact that children live in their own world and cannot be considered miniature adults. I also was realizing that they would listen more attentively to a puppet than to "the pastor" and that I was capable of a variety of styles and kinds of sermons. Then, I began to ask what constitutes a theologically-sound sermon. I wasn't doing better if I had caught their attention with something less than the gospel. Without sound theological principles I could never develop a sound preaching ministry with children. Thus, Part I of this book established a theological rationale for the sermons and stories that follow in Part II.

We have rationalized and deluded ourselves that a weekly children's sermon does not actually change lives, but theologically we know that nothing could be more important than sowing the seeds of the gospel early in life. We tell ourselves that children do not listen, that they are not mature enough to plumb the depths of the written Word, and that their time would be better spent in a

Sunday school classroom. Our excuses are endless and scarcely differ from the rationalization we use to pass over the ineffectiveness of our adult sermons. There ought to be an adage that sums up this problem, but since I could not find one I wrote my own:

> *If we cannot reach children*
> *with God's great love,*
> *What hope is there for hearts and minds*
> *iced over with age?*

I repeat, then, my hope that this handbook will stimulate more than it will settle matters, and that it will make us more willing and more capable of communicating the Love that has found us.

Part I

Laying A Firm Foundation

Introduction

This is a book for ministers, Christian educators, and anyone who bears the responsibility for telling the Good News to children. My particular interest is the worship setting where a place and time is set aside for proclaiming the love of God and the grace of Jesus Christ in such a way that it is *experienced* as love and grace. What makes this book unique is both what it is *not* and what it is. It is not the usual sampling of children's sermons (52 for 52 weeks or sermons that follow the liturgical calendar). These are readily available. My purpose is much broader. I look at all aspects of what it means to preach the Christian gospel to children. Most important is the critical eye that invites us to examine carefully what we are doing and could be doing. I do not know of any book devoted to the art and theology of gospel-telling. It is both astounding and disappointing that so little attention has been paid to this important subject. In short, this is not a book to provide you with sermons but to enable you to be more effective in the art and theology of children's sermons.

In the 1980s it was necessary to provide a rationale for children in worship. None is provided here because I presume children are recognized as integral to the life and worship of the church. John Westeroff's book, *Bringing up Children in the Christian Faith* (1980), was an important step forward because he argued so persuasively that Christian formation (as different from Christian education) happens in many contexts but none as important as corporate worship. Nevertheless, we must remind ourselves that children worship with the congregation not only because this is where they learn how to worship but because our worship is incomplete without them. I will say no more in this regard except to comment that there persists an attitude that even though we welcome children into the worship life of the congregation, there is only a half-hearted effort truly to integrate them.[1] The other significant change is the continued revival in liturgy. I cite as one example the popularity of "The Whole Life Curriculum" and the attention given to the integration of curriculum and worship, teaching and preaching. This shift is reflected in the section of this book titled "Liturgical vs. Secular Calendar." I know there is still a divide between those denominations with a strong liturgical tradition and those who still find it to be foreign. What unites us is a dissatisfaction with isolating the sermon, children and adults, from the total worship experience. We still have a distance to travel to integrate proclaiming and Christian formation in all of its various contexts. These are topics for a different book, but I am sensitive to them and address them indirectly.

The outline of this handbook is simple. I begin with what should be obvious but often isn't: It is darn difficult to proclaim the gospel so that it is *experienced* by children. Thus I look critically at the status quo over against participatory communication. Next, I clarify the purpose behind our gospel-telling. What makes this "moment" distinctive and transformative? The third section turns to the practical issues, such as where to begin and how to target the sermon. Because gospel-telling is an art or craft, the best I can do is provide the stimulation along with a few watch-words. Part II describes and illustrates a variety of ways to be a gospel-teller along with reflective notes. As you continue to read you will find that I am tough on myself and anyone who proclaims the gospel. I have included even a few of my failures in the sample sermons, for we should be persistent learners. And that is my parting word of advice — be critical of yourself and develop both a theology and a discipline that will make you the best gospel-teller this side or that side of the Mississippi.

It's Not All That Easy

A good children's sermon is simple, direct, dramatic, and participatory; it has a single purpose and enables the listener to experience God's love. A poor children's sermon is dull, rambling, uncreative, overly verbal, and moralistic; it is unfocused and entertaining rather than transformative. Having said this, the bar has been set very high but we must not become discouraged.

Moralism And Humanism

The Trap of Moralism. Moralism is such an easy trap to fall into! Without constant vigilance it simply happens, because we do not have before us a clear distinction between moralism and the Good News, between the indicative and the imperative. The indicative is the Good News that through Jesus Christ (his death and resurrection) each of us is invited into a new relationship with God. The imperative is the ethical response (both personal and social) that we make as that new creation begins to take root and blossom. The imperative is grounded in the indicative, not vice versa. Leander Keck, senior New Testament editor for the twelve-volume commentary *The New Interpreter's Bible* and former president of the Society of Biblical Literature, writes:

> *First of all, the nature of the moral life calls for more than attending to Jesus' teachings about what is and is not to be done, important though they are. The moral life is more than choosing and more than knowing what to choose and how to choose it ... In any case, the moral life pertains to the doer before it pertains to the deed....*
> — *Who is Jesus?*, p. 160

The writers of the Gospels narrate the story of Jesus by anchoring sayings and teachings of Jesus in the portrayal of his life and character. Thus, we need to guard against too many "should and should nots," especially so when left to dangle by themselves.

What good is a dozen "should" and "should nots" when they aren't the fruit of a life nurtured and grounded in Jesus my Savior?

Moralism is more of a trap when children are the congregation. While it is certainly true that children are in their formative years of developing a moral code, that is no excuse for detaching moral conduct from the Savior. If from the child's point of view the Good News is heard as sermons about being more respectful, industrious, kind, honest, and less wasteful, mean, selfish, and temperamental, then we have failed. In the hierarchy of virtues these would head almost every parent's list but they do not constitute the Kingdom Jesus preached. Even when we preach humility, compassion, peacemaking, joy, self-control, faithfulness, they are frequently treated as if they are possible in and of themselves. We know the Beatitudes and Paul's gifts of the Spirit are the fruit (imperative) of a tree planted and nurtured (indicative) in living for Christ. An adult parallel would be trying to scare cigarette smokers into kicking their habit or to expect alcoholics to stop drinking by sheer willpower and good intentions. What we learn from both of these imperative-first approaches is that we are only scared for a short time and then return to the old self, and individuals do not change unless their new formation is supported and encouraged by a community of believers. Alcoholics Anonymous begins with the premise that we are powerless and change results from the power of a Higher Being working a new creation within us. Moralism has the cart pulling the horse.

The goal of every children's sermon should be the grounding of God's expectation of what we can be in the communication of God's love and acceptance of who we are as children of God.

Unfortunately, most children's sermons aim at adjusting children's behavior instead of helping them form a relationship with God as they come to know Jesus. The negative consequence is that children experience love as law when they should be experiencing law as love; as Paul Scherer explains it, "Love experienced as Law ceases to be love. Law experienced as Love ceases

18

to be Law" (*The Word God Sent*, p. 15). Practically speaking, this does not mean that every sermon should have as its sole purpose the conversion of the child. There are good reasons why a gospel-telling is not followed with an altar call. But it does mean that every children's sermon with a moral imperative should place that moral injunction in a context where it is perceived as an act of love rather than duty. In the sermon "Overcoming Temptation," how easy it would have been to present the experience of temptation and neglect to include the Christian antidote (prayer). If Jesus had come to make us good, then persuasion would be our objective. But since Jesus came to demonstrate God's great love, our goal is to prepare the heart to be loved by God.

The Trap of Humanism. Humanism is the sibling of moralism. It too is a trap waiting to be sprung. If moralism is the ever present danger of confusing the gospel with character building, humanism is the ever present danger of confusing the gospel with the wisdom of the ages or parental/pastoral advice. The Bible is, of course, filled with the best kind of worldly wisdom, and the preacher has no difficulty in finding a suitable text to support humanistic truths. But the result is again paramount to separating the message from the Messenger.

Moralism often arises when we are trying to make practical the teachings of Jesus, while humanism results from trying to be overly original and "hip." If moralism is the pitfall of conservatism, then humanism is the undertow of liberalism. Just because a sermon is drawn from Scripture does not mean it is exempt from moralism and humanism. More often than not we have removed the text from its fuller narrative context and used it as a springboard. Fairy tales, fables, and most children's stories are humanistic. This does not necessarily make them unsuitable as a starting place for a children's sermon; they simply cannot be the message and if they are not the message, there must be a very good reason to begin here.

The gospel without Jesus Christ is like a car without a motor: it looks attractive as long as it is standing still, but as soon as one tries to drive it, its fatal flaw is discovered. Likewise, children will find humanistic sermons interesting and enjoyable but completely useless outside of church where wisdom quickly turns into expediency. Unless an individual has a living relationship with Christ, the imperative to return evil with good and to overcome hate with love will only be lessons in frustration. No matter how it is dressed up, worldly wisdom will always be advice about how to make it in this world. In proclaiming God's foolishness (1 Corinthians 1:18) humanism and moralism will forever be attractive alternatives, but we know we have sold our children a "bill of goods" soon to be found wanting.

Simile, Allegory, Metaphor, Literalism

A simile is a concise figure of speech that directly compares two unrelated things to indicate a shared likeness between them, usually by the use of "like" or "as." For example, "All we *like* sheep have gone astray" (Isaiah 53:6). An allegory necessarily involves the listener in a decoding process but one that is more complex and symbolic. A story is told, a pictorial representation is given, that suggests a central truth, thus augmenting and deepening the meaning of the lesson. The parable of the sower (Mark 4:3-8), for example, preserves a story which had become allegorized in the classical sense; its point-for-point interpretation follows (vv. 14-20; cf. Ezekiel 17:3-10, 11-21).[2] Both similes and allegories depend upon a form of conceptual thinking we know as analogical where an inference is drawn based on the assumption that if two things are alike in some respect, then they must be alike in other respects. The insight into their alikeness in their difference is what make similes and allegories enlightening.

Like a simile and an allegory, a metaphor vitalizes speech by juxtaposing two *unrelated* things in order to make one or both more striking. Unlike an allegory or a simile, a metaphor accomplishes its goal by making the comparison implicitly. When Saint Paul speaks of Christ crucified as a stumbling block unto the Jews (1 Corinthians 1:23), he is forming a metaphor because the meaning that is implied depends upon bringing together the idea of the Messiah and death by crucifixion — each acceptable in its own right but in combination certainly unthinkable to a Jewish population awaiting a King who would sit on David's throne. Of course, this metaphor could be extended in many ways by way of a story or a parable.

A simile most often uses the conjunction "like," while a metaphor employs the predicate "is." Thus, we have several levels of abstraction as we move from simple description to simile, allegory, and metaphor.

God *is* strong and gentle.

God is strong and gentle *like* a shepherd.

The Lord *is* my *shepherd.*

Consider the analogy in the following Easter sermon for children. In trying to explain the meaning of Easter (rather than trying to create the experience of Easter), the minister said something to this effect. "Just *like* the egg that is broken open and out comes a chick, so the tomb was broken open and Jesus came out." The analogy involves a complex decoding process of analogical thinking.

egg = tomb

chick = Jesus

This is a lot for a little mind to digest and if digested it makes for a lot of strange conclusions. The resurrection of Jesus defies explanation and thus invites analogies and metaphors. One of the two Easter sermons in the book is to some extent analogical but is notably more experiential and meant to evoke awe and wonderment. The alternative is simple direct speech (see the reflection note in the sermon, "Baa-Baa"). You judge which is the better.

It is necessary to distinguish between literalism and direct speech. Literalism is a form of speech or interpretation where exaggeration, metaphor, or double meanings are prohibited. It expects the speech, written or spoken, to be taken for just what it is, its plain sense. Direct speech is described by the family therapist Virginia Satir as "leveling" where all parts of the message are going in the same direction (*Peoplemaking*, pp. 72-79). Leveling is contrasted with loaded messages with multiple meanings, some conscious and some unconscious, where the voice is saying one thing but the rest of you is feeling and communicating something else. It would seem that literalism and direct speech are the same because they are about the plain sense of what is being said. The difference is that literalism — especially in the way younger children think — is fraught with complications that mar the plain sense. What is the literal sense of "the Lord is my shepherd" or even "the Lord is like a shepherd"? The child probably does not know what a shepherd is like and so the analogy is not immediately useful or understandable in its plain sense. A story is needed to show what a shepherd does (see "Baa-Baa"). The difficulty with literalism is that we do not always know when to take the words literally or when they imply a simile or an analogy or need to be interpreted symbolically or metaphorically; and this is as true of Scripture as everyday speech. If as adults we are not sure what the intended meaning is, then children will surely be uncertain or mistaken about what is said literally when that is not what is meant because a strict literal sense is nonsense. Since younger children often think literally, they hear a literal meaning when this is not the intended meaning.

When the moment of gospel-telling comes, you, as the proclaimer, need to be aware of your primary mode of communication. This is complicated by three factors: your understanding of the biblical mode of communication, the mode that is appropriate for the age of the children, and the type of message you are delivering. Almost everyone agrees the Bible includes simile, allegory, metaphor, historical, theological, poetic, and narrative forms of speech. Disagreement arises about which form is being used by the author, such as in the Noah story. The one safe conclusion is that no one form is so predominant that we should feel obligated to use it all the time. The second certain consensus is that children are not very adept or even have the capacity for the kind of abstraction that simile, allegory, and metaphor require. A separate discussion, "Targeting Your Sermon," will go into this matter in greater detail. I would add nevertheless that literalism has its own particular pitfalls and that imaginative language is not necessarily inappropriate (see "Overhearing The Gospel"). But as a rule the conversation that works best is the kind that is personal, direct, and level. Third, and here we can learn from the biblical writers, different types of messages require different modes of communication. Jesus' use of parables was effective, for instance, because of its indirection (catching the listener off-guard). The sense of awe and wonderment (the wholly Other) cannot be communicated literally because words cannot contain the mystery of God or the amazement of God's grace. Some messages will be direct, concrete, and simple while others may be suggestive, double-edged, poetic, even paradoxical because as human beings we respond to different modes of communication at different times and ages of our lives. As proclaimers we are responsible for being aware of the level of meaning and the means of communication we are employing.

Object Lessons

The object lesson has become the preferred menu for children's sermons by default. I may be unfairly critical of object lessons because they have a momentum toward moralism and allegory. The object is intended to ground the lesson in a reality children understand (see e.g., "God Doesn't Make Telephone Calls" where the telephone recreates an experience we are familiar with). When Kathleen Fannin accepted the role of gospel-teller in her church, she relates the advice she received and took to be gospel. "A second bit of wisdom was offered by an eight-year-old when I was talking with his mother in the grocery store. 'Don't *ever* do a children's sermon without a visual aid' " (*Cows In Church: 52 Biblically Based Children's Sermons*). More often than not the object serves as a springboard, an attention getter, a starting place (see the sermon "Breakfast Of Champions"). It does happen occasionally that the object is the lesson (see the sermon "An Apple A Day"). The object may also be used to illustrate or demonstrate, for example, when the air in a balloon is compared to the Holy Spirit (see "Adding A Drop Of Love" where the drop of food coloring is illustrative). In a pure object lesson, the object is indispensable and because it is indispensable an analogy or moral is often forthcoming. Some form of reasoning is needed to get from the object to the lesson. A "lesson," however, is not the same as "proclamation." I could point out that Jesus did not utilize object lessons but that would be unfair, because we do not know how he interacted with children except to love them and include them.

23

What we do know is that Jesus' method of communication was direct, distinctive, participatory, and involved "overhearing." I have developed what I think is a healthy skepticism about object lessons because they are too much about mind and not enough about heart.

What objects do accomplish is to make speech more concrete by the use of visual aids. Words alone can be boring and ineffective, especially so with children who have limited patience with abstract thinking. The exception to this rule is the story form because it has a plot (a reason to listen) and because it is personal (it is about someone I know, someone I would like to know, and myself).

The Misuse Of Biblical Heroes And Stories

If only gospel-telling were as easy as retelling the stories found in the Old and New Testaments. When a children's sermon is a familiar biblical narrative told in an interesting way, the underlying assumption is that children will assimilate the Christian faith by way of familiarity. A number of difficulties, however, must be recognized. First, most biblical stories were written for adults and are situated in a narrative context. When removed from their theological context and simply retold they are likely to be misappropriated by children. Children may be told about Adam and Eve, Noah and his ark, the crossing of the Red Sea, Jonah and the whale, David and Goliath, Zacchaeus, and the Good Samaritan, but they are usually left to devise their own interpretations of these stories. Children internalize these accounts but often with horrendous results.

Telling the Adam and Eve narrative as a literal story, for example, may result in banishing sin to some faraway time, localizing it in an unknown place, associating it with picking fruit or nudity, or confirming the cultural bias that snakes and women are not to be trusted. If we abide by a literal interpretation, we must be aware of the two extremes — hearing it as literally true or as a fairy tale, and depending upon the age of the children this is what we should expect. The story is heard as something that happened a long time ago in a faraway place with a talking snake. Our real obligation is to teach children that sin is what happens in back-yards and playgrounds. It isn't easy to make the connection be-tween Adam and Eve and the inevitability and universality of sin for a seven-year-old. I suspect this is one reason why fewer and fewer children's sermons utilize biblical stories or depend upon the Bible at all.

If one is inclined toward reading biblical stories as historical accounts, another set of difficulties arises. One is drawn into a succession of explanations the biblical writers never intended: how did Noah distinguish between male and female turtles, how did Jonah find sufficient oxygen to breathe, why didn't Goliath just squash David? While younger children bask in fantasy and make-believe, older children are intent upon sorting out fact from fic-tion. While children do not have to contend with historical criti-cism, they do become confused or mystified by a welter of dis-jointed accounts that seem totally unrelated to their lives. It is well to keep in mind that each biblical story was part of a larger story and it was the larger narrative that enabled the part to be meaning-ful. The Adam-Eve story is part of the prologue (Genesis 1-11) of a much longer narrative of Israel and God, and Jonah is not about survival techniques but how to love (not just tolerate) foreigners.

Certain biblical stories are great fun for anyone with a vivid imagination. As children we delighted in picture books of Adam and Eve in the Garden of Paradise, a box full of animals along with Noah and his wife, the strong right hand of Moses parting the Red Sea, a song about Zacchaeus in his sycamore tree. But as a child matures, these stories are relegated to the not-so-important corner of the mind. If we wait to communicate the theological significance of biblical stories, we wait too long and we must live with the consequences of our mental laziness. Children become adults faster than we think, and if we avoid explaining the story of Jonah, there is a good chance they will grow up believing the story is outrageous for the wrong reason. It is not so difficult for chil-dren to understand the prejudice of a man who did not like for-eigners — those Ninevites — and what it means to struggle with the God who redraws the line of inclusion/exclusion. They have the capacity to realize the Hebrews preserved the story of Jonah not as a fairy tale or fable, but as a story that shows how God's mercy overwhelms us. Certainly this isn't a message for adults only, but when it is proclaimed to children it isn't easy.

Storytellers, beware! Those very features that make a story interesting and arresting also divert us from and cloud the life-and-death meaning they were originally meant to dramatize. When the stories we tell happened long ago, focus upon their theological intent and try not to imply something that will later lead to confusion or need to be relearned.

Biblical heroes represent another briar patch. The Bible is not the first place children go in order to find their heroes. Frequently heroes like Moses and Daniel are singled out for their heroic deeds (parting the Red Sea, escaping the fiery furnace, etc.). The attraction of super heroes wears thin as children are forced to be realistic about life. They serve a certain need for fantasy and escapism but that need is quickly in conflict with a need to succeed, to be liked, to do well. Living in a culture so saturated with superstars drawn from sports and music, everyone else seems irrelevant. Biblical heroes, as they are usually depicted, never disappoint because they are idealizations frozen in time. Sports heroes and music legends, on the other hand, attract a following because of the cultural values they embody, most of them not Christian values.

Nevertheless, biblical figures should not be dismissed. They should be presented with the same honesty they are portrayed in scripture. The "movers and shakers" of various biblical narratives know a thing or two about sin, doubt, shame, limitations, handicaps. As someone who has struggled with his own handicap, stuttering, I appreciate the heroes who persevered "in spite of." Saint Paul does speak of finishing the race, not being first. It is curious how Zacchaeus has been singled out among many New Testament figures to be popularized. Like Johnny Appleseed, he has become a natural part of childhood memories, because of a catchy song, colorful pictures, and the ease with which we identify with him. My hunch is that Zacchaeus has become an all-time favorite because children can identify with the feeling of being small and disliked. (Just try having them identify with "the woman with a flow of blood" or one of the several lepers.) Children — especially boys — identify with David the giant-killer for similar reasons. Though not very old or very big, David put the bully in his place. But herein lies the danger. Without a lot of additional help from adults, children get carried away with the image of the little man in a sycamore tree or the boy with a slingshot. (What better justification for having your very own weapon of destruction?) In the final analysis, identification is the name of the game here. These stories need to be fleshed out. On his rise to glory, Kind David is loved by all (except for Saul) and thereby falls in love with himself. Zacchaeus was also rich, powerful (a tax collector), and despised. His salvation is the story of how one lacking in stature (both literally and metaphorically) is "made tall" in the eyes of those who had despised him (and the line of who is "in" and who is "out" is redrawn). The very same heroes who are portrayed as bigger than life are the very same heroes who experience the grace of God when they are brought low (mostly by their own actions). There probably isn't a child or teenager alive who hasn't aspired to be a super hero, but I don't see them identifying with figures from the Bible. On the other hand, they know and will know loneliness, rejection, guilt, failure, doubt; I hope they will have heard of a story or two of someone who has also known these and was able to keep the faith (see the sermon "Breakfast Of Champions").

Very little irritates me more than the annual massacre of the story of the Good Samaritan. He has become the paradigm of virtue because he stopped to help one in need as others passed by on the other side. But do children realize the story turns on the fact that the Samaritan was a half-breed, both racially and religiously? This story was not originally heard as imperative ("Go thou and do likewise") but as indicative (the neighbor who loves more than me is a Samaritan!). The parable (not cute, moralistic anecdotes but stories of reversal) is Jesus' answer to the question about the limits of love (Who can be called my neighbor? Could a Samaritan be called "good"?). In the echo story included in this handbook, you will find the usual emphasis on helping someone who is hurt, but you will also find a frequently omitted "hook" that the Good Samaritan is a geek or whoever in your setting is the last person on earth you would want to be your neighbor. Children perceive this as a contradiction, yet it is this very contradiction that gives the story its impact and carries its radical message about the nature of Christian love. Although this may seem like a minor point, it makes a difference between a sentimental story of a do-gooder and a shocking account of a "loser" who did not pass by on the other side.

The biblical stories were not told and retold because of their historical content or the validity of their scientific explanations; they remained relevant and vital because they provided identity to the people who "passed them on" (tradition). As ones who are called to pass on that same tradition, we confront the danger of being literal and uncreative in order to be biblical, that is, telling the old, old story as if it were a body of information to be learned.

Participatory Communication

In summary, utilize leveling where everything flows in the same direction except for those instances where a conscious decision is made to be disruptive and suggestive in order to surprise the listener and turn his/her known world upside down. There is another aspect of communication we must take into account. Listen to the sage advise from one our country's best preachers, Fred B. Craddock.

> In the first place, the Bible addresses the community of faith and is not a collection of theological and ethical arguments to persuade atheists or adherents of other religions.
>
> Secondly, it is generally characteristic of the Bible not to repeat a story verbatim and from that story draw lessons and exhortations appropriate to the particular audience, but rather to retell the story in such a way that it properly addresses the hearers.
>
> — Overhearing the Gospel, p. 66

As preachers we try to be engaging (as distinct from being interesting but that too). When we excite children we always engage adults, but the converse is not necessarily true. So how do we

28

engage children? This book offers many suggestions but they can be summarized in the phrase "participatory communication." And that is what makes our task so difficult. We have mentioned the universal impression that the *object* is the way to captivate children. In Part II there are six different kinds of gospel-tellings: let's pretend, visual demonstrations, dramatic participation, pantomime and echo, storytelling, and puppets. While dramatic participation is the purest form of participatory communication, all the sermons have this as their aim.

Participatory communication is based upon the following Learning Pyramid.[3]

Children learn

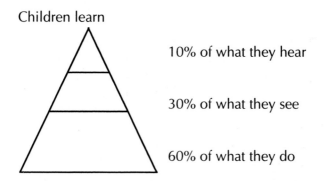

10% of what they hear

30% of what they see

60% of what they do

We know from practical experience that the greater an individual's involvement in a learning situation, the greater the degree of retention. For example, the reader is more likely to remember the information just presented if he receives the visual stimulus of the pyramid rather than just the stimulus of a long descriptive paragraph. Similarly, learning to ride a bicycle is a formative experience (in contrast to a learning experience) because it requires the total participation of the individual.

Because of the nature of their development, the span of concentration, and their exposure to mass media, children have a built-in screen against excessive verbal communication. In their early years they learn as much through touching, tasting, feeling, and observing as they do by hearing and seeing. Just consider the miracle of how children learn what is basic to their development: crawling, walking, trusting, a sense of "self," a sense of "other,"

29

what is "fair," etc. The complex ability to use language comes last and it too is not just about hearing words but hearing within a context. *The use of "props" connected with words in order to make something more concrete is not the epitome of effective preaching.* In fact, we never reach the apex until we approximate the experience of riding a bicycle or learning to swim. We are, after all, talking about Christian formation and transformation — the patterns of living that arise from our personal, firsthand experience of living for Jesus and Jesus living in us. Trying to explain something that is essentially experiential using abstract concepts which can only be communicated verbally is not acceptable. Participatory communication is at the other end of the spectrum: it is about doing, touching, tasting, feeling, smelling, seeing, and hearing in order to experience what will be serviceable. In the sermon "An Apple A Day," children do all of these and any words spoken are secondary. Gospel-tellings give us the freedom to do all kinds of crazy, fun stuff that is truly interesting because it is participatory.

The Broadway hit musical *Godspell* is such a delight because it presents biblical material (parables, sayings, narrative, and action) in a variety of fresh ways. I selected the sermons in this handbook because they also suggest a variety of ways to preach the gospel other than the usual stand-up monologue delivered with an object in hand. As ministers and teachers of children (as compared to adults), we have the distinct advantage of knowing immediately how effective we are. If hands and feet begin to fidget, and heads begin to turn and side-bar conversations spring up, then we know we have lost them because the communication has been a monologue. I was once surprised during a children's sermon when a boy of seven flashed me a particular sign we had learned in Vacation Bible School two weeks earlier (the thumb pointed horizontally and the index finger pointing vertically). At that time I was wondering if any of the eighty restless children were engaged. I knew then at least one had picked up the visual clue and I hoped he remembered the verse: Love God with all your heart (vertical finger) and your neighbor as yourself (horizontal finger).

Here is the appropriate place to take a critical look at the question/answer approach to participation. We ask a question and the children answer (the Socratic method). For some children — those who do well in school — this methodology will capture them and they will be participants in the gospel-telling. As Vince Lombardi, the successful football coach of the Green Bay Packers, said about passing: Three things can happen and two aren't good. First, when you ask questions, children begin to "go fish" for the right answer. Second, when you ask questions there is a high probability you will be sidetracked. If you are looking for a humorous moment, then go ahead and take your chances. What we must guard against is the over dependence upon questions and answers as the primary way we try to make communication participatory.

Most congregations have resources that certainly should be tapped. Among the members are artists, musicians, engineers, actors, and storytellers who are usually willing to assist in a special project. In a church in New Jersey, a high school shop teacher had put together a working robot which the minister used effectively for a number of children's sermons. Although such creativity is a great thing, we must make sure that it does not displace the gospel message itself.

The Purpose Behind Our Gospel-Telling

The Distinctive Character Of The Gospel

What are we doing in the moment called gospel-telling? It is easy to be caught up with the content and style of one's gospel-telling and lose sight of what we ultimately hope to achieve. We witness and proclaim the Good News of God's grace and love revealed in Jesus the Christ. Speaking more practically we may find ourselves from Sunday to Sunday engaged in one of the following:

Enlightenment — wake up and smell the roses, be thankful, rejoice.

Teaching — this is what it means to be a disciple, a church member, a Christian.

Be a better person — keep the Ten Commandments, the Boy Scout Law; bear the good fruit worthy of a Christian.

Vocation — as Jesus grew in wisdom and stature and in favor with God, so you need to become a mature Christian claiming your Christian identity.

Conversion — change your ways (repent) because the gate to Hell is wide and the way is easy.

Different children's sermons will have different purposes. When all is said and done I return to this baptismal question: Will you (the parents and the congregation) shape your child's life in the image of Christ by nurturing him/her in the life of the church? As we reflect upon what it means to share these gospel moments with children, shaping and forming are a more holistic understanding of what we hope will be taking place as months turn into years. At work behind the scene is Saint Paul's encouragement: "Do not be conformed to this world but let your minds be remade and your whole nature be transformed" (Romans 12:2). We are preparing children, to use words from the Gospel of John, to be "in the world but not of the world." In order not to be co-opted by the world, we arm them with heroes, stories, images, songs, experiences, values, disciplines, and practices that plant them in the reign of God's

33

love. Every day and in every way there are claims being made upon their personhood. Being under continual assault by the secular world, children need to re-experience their baptism, to know of God's claim upon their lives and the joy of living a Christ-filled life.

The responsibility for a theologically-sound gospel-telling would not be so demanding if we could just parrot the culture. As we prepare to create experiences of being loved by God and to effect Christian formation, the questions become what values, what behavior, what love. And the obvious answer is those values and behaviors that are distinctively Christian. There is a body of cultural values that is often confused with what is essential to the gospel — values such as friendliness, honesty, kindness, cooperation, respect. Then there are the values that are thoroughly Christian but shorn of their distinctive Christian identity in a secular society — values such as forgiveness, humility, perseverance, hospitality, joy. There are also values we share with Judaism: the Ten Commandments and the Great Commandment. Should all of these be taught? Yes, of course. Should these be manifested behaviors that children see and imitate? Of course. My word of caution though is this: Be clear about what is distinctively Christian, for the time we spend with children is so very precious and limited.

In my pre-marriage counseling I begin (after getting acquainted) with this question: What is distinctive about Christian marriage? Why come to me, an ordained minister, instead of a justice of the peace? The questions are meant to provoke a particular discussion about what we are doing here. Usually, with considerable leading on my part, we look at these values: adoration and praise, confession, offering of substance and self, a word from God that is not out own (Scripture and homily), benediction (blessing). We then talk about these acts of worship and why they should be included in a Christian wedding service and a Christian marriage. I continue this "teaching moment" by pointing out that preschool children learn these values and behaviors in the same way that preschoolers learn everything else, namely, by participation, observation, learning "on the go," and their five senses. Children and adults, but especially children, learn what it is to be a Christian (these behaviors and values) because they experience God's love as it enacted within a Christian community, for that is why Christians do not worship alone or at home.

It isn't necessarily the conduct but the motivation that is distinctively Christian. It was Reinhold Niebuhr who argued that there is no such thing as a Christian action, only Christians who perform Christ-like acts. From a different perspective Dietrich Bonhoeffer believed in the validity of a nonreligious way of being in the world. "It is not some religious act which makes a Christian what he is," he wrote, "but participation in the suffering of God in the life of the world" (*Letters and Papers from Prison*). The conclusion is this: we not only model a distinctively Christian way of being in the world, we bring-to-speech the reason we do what we do. Because children are in the midst of intense developmental processes — especially trying to discover who they are and what they are good for — we proclaim the reason for the season is Jesus Christ and that reason is Someone who has touched our hearts.

Integrating The Sermon Into Worship And Life
The children's message should neither be isolated nor obtrusive. Every service of corporate worship should be planned around a central theme, and the children's homily should represent a development of that theme for a particular age group. When the children's sermon is not part of a general theme, even the most well thought-out message only reinforces the assumption that it is a nice sidelight that is occasionally included. It is more difficult to develop an effective message for children when we have unlimited freedom. If we try to develop a great idea or a creative gimmick of our choice, we often find our wheels spinning. The Scripture text that is the basis for the adult sermon should be the foundation of the children's sermon for practical and theological reasons.

The children's sermon should connect with more than the immediate context of the Sunday worship service (see "The Bigger Picture"). The pastor should be aware of the subject matter being taught in the Sunday school and the Director of Christian Education should be aware of what is being preached and why. Those curriculums that have common texts and themes for all ages make this goal easier but not easy. Because there is more than one text and many ways to develop those texts, it is difficult to achieve a singleness of purpose. And yet simply being aware of the curriculum enables the pastor to avoid a total separation between Sunday worship and the church school. With careful planning, ministers and educators can develop the morning lesson as an experience which will subsequently be developed in the classroom.

We are responsible for continually searching out ways to reinforce the gospel beyond the confines of the sanctuary. The sermon "My One-tenth Box" is an example of learning that begins in the sanctuary but is meant to be continued as a family pattern. This book offers several stories and demonstrations that are purposefully left unfinished, because they are meant to be extended and completed outside the church buildings (e.g., "Yesterday I Stomped On A Frog" and "A Prince In Disguise"). Although I haven't included a serial, it is possible to begin one and let it continue for several Sundays, as long as each part stands on its own. The proclaimer should not be hesitant about repeating a particular theological theme.

Supporting One Central Point

It seems so obvious that I will be brief. Each sermon has one central experience and everything flows toward or away from that experience. One is often tempted to teach several truths, especially when we have hit upon a creative idea. In the sermon "All The Glue In The World," one child is invited to destroy a beautiful flower while another child is challenged to restore it to its original beauty. Because this sermon excites several important themes — good stewardship, the sacredness of life, evidence of God's existence — it was tempting to mention all three truths, particularly because the drama cannot be repeated. The alternative is to construct the proclamation carefully so that it can be effective at more than one level at the same time. Instead of indulging in overkill, or using an approach that forces everyone to follow one logical path, develop the sermon so that older children and adults can intuitively perceive a certain richness which they can pursue later (see "Overhearing The Gospel").

As part of my own discipline and by way of example, I have included a one-sentence summary of each sermon in this handbook. But bear in mind that a summary and a conclusion are not identical. Conclusions often result from the flow of events while summaries should always be clarified ahead of time. Only after you outline a sermon can you examine it for unity, weed out what is extraneous and distracting, and sharpen its singular purpose. Although most of us do not write out a children's sermon, we lose a great deal if we do not write down a summary statement. Do this before Saturday night so there is time to percolate a text and an idea and turn it into an experience.

Liturgical vs. Secular Calendar

The minister faces the choice whether it is better to favor the secular or the liturgical calendar. An argument can be made for both. There are certain secular events and dates that are difficult to ignore: the beginning of the school year, Halloween, Thanksgiving, Martin Luther King Jr. Day, Boy/Girl Scout Sunday, Holocaust Remembrance Day, Memorial Day, Mother's Day, Father's Day, and July 4. There are invariably noteworthy events in the life of the church: baptisms, significant anniversaries, stewardship Sunday, reception of new members, Habitat Sunday, CROP walks, One Great Hour of Sharing, etc. Halloween is a case in point. It has its historical roots in All Saints' Day and should be celebrated by Christians in association with the remembrance of the saints who have died. The liturgical year has a number of Jewish festivals and secular (pagan) "holidays" that have been Christianized (Feast of Weeks = Pentecost, winter solstice = Christmas). Now the reverse has happened where the culture has secularized Christian festivals. Because the process of secularization is so prevalent, worship leaders may not want to miss the opportunity to teach and reclaim Halloween as our own. On the other hand, Thanksgiving is a secular feast day but it can be an opportunity to recover the

distinctive aspects of a Judeo-Christian understanding of stewardship (we are a thankful people, not just thankful for this and that).
Every holiday and remembrance mentioned above is worthy of
our attention. The issue is whether they should constitute the calendar, and thus the continuity, we follow as proclaimers.

On the other hand we are a peculiar people with a particular
way of telling time and this is embodied within the liturgical year.
In the more liturgical traditions and where the Common Lectionary
is prominent, the decision has been made. The Sabbath along with
the liturgical calendar provide the governing structure for our corporate life as a worshiping people. The Sabbath and the move-
ment from Advent through Pentecost (or Trinity Sunday) is itself a
way to tell our Story. It becomes our ally to resist being conformed
to this world. There are some practical compromises that can be
made but a mishmash of both approaches is, for the most part,
unsatisfactory. At the very least, children can help change the
antependiums for the pulpit and lectern when the seasons change.
Attention can be drawn to a change in stoles, and a liturgical calendar with a pointer can be displayed in the sanctuary. The choice
then is whether it is more effective to counter the prevailing culture by reinterpreting the secular calendar or by consistently telling the Story within the framework of the liturgical calendar. My
vote is for the latter because the Story we proclaim needs a structure and the liturgical calendar is the best framework we have.
Those other remembrances can be properly attended to, for example, as we pray together.

The Bigger Picture

What would it look like to see an entire year's sermons spread
out before you? The question invokes a critical reflection not usually considered.[4] It also returns us to the fundamental issue of what
we hope is happening when we practice gospel-telling. It would
be the rare bird who planned his or her children's sermons for the
year. If such planning happens it is for the adult sermons with
some collateral effect if the children's sermon follows the same
message. But who would ever think of outlining a year's worth of
children's sermons? Very few because of the presumption that

38

gospel-telling should be spontaneous and serendipitous. And so it should be; but when considering our proclamation over the course of the year, should we be content with pearls without a string to hang them on?

From another era Harry Emerson Fosdick practiced a philosophy that "every sermon should have for its main business the solving of some problem — a vital, important problem, puzzling minds, burdening consciences, distracting lives." Regardless of what you think of that focus, he had one. Since we do not think of children has having "spiritual problems," do we think of them as having "growing-up problems"? Should this be our focal point? As worthy as this might be, it does little to remedy the jack-in-the-box effect of pulling out of your hat (brown bag) some new trick each Sunday.

It is not my place to suggest how you might focus your gospel-telling or even to recommend a yearly plan. But at least consider your various contexts: the world as seen through the eyes of children, the mission statement of your church, goals established by the leadership of your congregation, specific Christian education objectives, reinforcing the Sunday school curriculum, a take-home message for children to discuss with their parents and siblings, learning and experiencing the drama of the Christian Story.[5] Let there be some sense of coherence and continuity in the midst of impulsive, impromptu acts of random gospel-tellings.

Using Scripture And Prayer Appropriately

How do ministers and laity communicate that this messages is not their own but God's as recorded in Scripture? If a children's sermon ends up being humanistic or moralistic, attaching a biblical text or praying over it will not redeem it. On the other hand, a sermon that is thoroughly biblical in its content and purpose but says nothing about its origin and motivation runs the risk of separating the message from the Messenger. As ministers and teachers of the Word, we should do nothing to add to the impression that many children already harbor — the Bible is what adults read, Noah's Ark is an original Walt Disney creation, the story of Johnny Appleseed is an Old Testament Story.

I personally find it too artificial and ritualistic to begin or end always with a reading of Scripture or a prayer. Over time scripture and prayer become viewed as appendages, and for the most part that is what they are. We are also guilty of introducing a scripture text and subsequently ignoring it. Stories, sayings, and teachings from the Bible are not duly acknowledged. Prayers serve to dismiss the children to their classes. I ask: What do these actions and omissions teach children about scripture and prayer? Let us remember that we teach by what we do and by what we do not do.

The issue is how to be explicit without being overly explicit. The sermons "A Prince In Disguise" and "What To Do With A Chocolate Chip Cookie?" illustrate the quandry we face. Theologically speaking, neither sermon needs a biblical reference to validate it. Yet to omit the Prince's origin in Matthew's story of the Great Judgment in chapter 25 leaves the children in doubt about the story's model. If the minister is overly explicit, that is, if he reads an appropriate scriptural text about justice and hunger before he gives out one or two cookies, then he dissipates the degree of conflict the sermon needs. Likewise, when we pray to the effect: "Dear God, let me summarize since some children may not have been paying attention," we reduce praying to asking God for one more chance to get it right.

I do make it a rule that when I quote scripture or repeat a saying of Jesus, to do so from a Bible in hand and not from memory (and of course not from notes). Even though we may be entirely certain where our inspiration comes from, it may not always be evident to the children who sit next to us. When we pray let our aim be to model prayer as best we understand it and let those prayers be sincere prayers of thanksgiving and confession, intercession and petition. In this book I have not usually included my prayers because they are spontaneous. When children are not present for the "prayers of the people" (pastoral prayer), a prayer "for the children" may be offered, that is, a prayer on behalf of these children and for the children of the world. In the sermon "Overcoming Temptation," it was perfectly natural to pray within the context of the sermon. Prayer is prayer because it brings us into relationship with God and from that relationship we receive the courage and hope to live out the gospel.

The Art Of Gospel-Telling

Some of us are naturally talented and others of us are naturally terrified of gospel-telling. In this section I will make practical suggestions to overcome your fears and hesitancies while energizing whatever talents we possess. Because we do have different talents and interests to employ, there will be a variety of styles and sermon forms.

Where To Begin

The customary approach is to begin with the scripture text/s and its development into an adult sermon, then, to reduce it to a children's message. What is laudable is the unity it provides to the service of worship. It also helps to root the children's message in Scripture. The difficulty this approach engenders is the "reduction" it embraces. Here I would ask ministers and teachers to make a 180-degree turn. Instead of developing the gospel-telling from the top down, work from the bottom up. Don't reduce an adult theme — most likely drawn from a passage meant for adults — in order to make it understandable for children. Begin with the same Scripture text and think and feel as a child does. The reason for the reversal is this: Children live in a unique world and children of different ages inhabit different worlds. Magazines such as *Time* and *Newsweek* have recently featured articles about how the brains of adolescents are different. Perhaps something new is being learned as science maps the brain, but parents and teachers have always known teenagers to be a "species" unto their own. The same is true for children, though adults characteristically want to think of children as pint-size, underdeveloped adults.

I begin with the scripture passage; while this seems matter-of-course it is not always practiced. The alternative is to begin with the object or a creative idea or the hook which will catch their attention. From a practical point of view and personal experience, this is a sea of choices too big and the result is that I expend too much time trying to decide which fish to reel in. Begin with the text and then revert to being a child — if not your own childhood then children you know. Interpret it as they would hear it. Ask how it is relevant for the world they inhabit. You may find that the message is very different from its adult application. Resist the temptation to say something simply in the children's sermon that is meant for the entire congregation. Yes, we have all heard how much adults appreciate the children's message which says more about our adult preaching than our children's sermons (see "Overhearing The Gospel" for a discussion of working on several levels at the same time). Take the time to write down in a phrase the intent of the gospel-telling. Give yourself time for creative juices to flow. This rules out a Sunday morning run-about or prayers for divine intervention. Give some thought to the target age group.

A word about creativity. It can't be forced. It needs time to "brew." Rather than rushing about to find an appropriate object, ask what medium of communication is most appropriate for the message itself. A pantomime, for example, is fitting for the sermon "Overcoming Temptation," because temptation is an experience that happens in the quite recesses of our hearts and minds. If I choose the form first, without considering its relationship to my message, I may still be wondering what I really want to say on Sunday morning, or the sermon may come across as disconnected because the form (the creative impulse) and the content do not connect.

Developing Your Style And Tone

To a very significant degree the medium is the message, and in this instance the proclaimer is the primary medium. Fred Craddock states it eloquently: "When we respond we respond to *someone*" (*Overhearing the Gospel*, p. 43). A most revealing exercise is to ask a friend to observe you. Ask her to block out your voice in order to be more sensitive to other stimuli; the next Sunday have her screen out all visual stimuli in order to attend to the verbal quality of your sermon. In this way your observer will grasp a good sense of both the verbal and nonverbal situation *you are creating*. While you cannot control everything in the immediate environment, you can shape the context and yourself to affect a particular tone and style. In one way or another you will need the feed-back of an observer.

Tone has to do with more than just delivery. Ultimately, it raises questions concerning identity: *who you are* (How do you feel about yourself? How do you project yourself?), *who you are in relationship to your audience* (you are big, and they are small; you know it all, so they must learn from you; you are very much like them, yet very different; you are father/mother; you are intimate, you are distant); and *who you are together* (they are the exposed ones sitting in front; we are the ones having a private conversation; we are the ones sharing stories about God and ourselves). You may think of yourself as a "natural" with children, or you may feel awkward with them. Regardless of the validity of such a generalization, you can change many things once you begin to pay attention to the situation you create by the little things you do or don't do.

To a certain extent you will be limited by the particular physical circumstances of your sanctuary; but reexamine these factors, for they are important. To shape the more immediate context of the gospel-telling moment, start by asking what you want to communicate about yourself and this shared time with the children of your church. It will then be possible for you to affect such factors as physical distance (standing or sitting, at the same height or not), children facing the congregation or not facing the congregation, your dress (Do you always wear a robe or a stole and if so why?), the quality of your voice (Is it any different in this context? What does it project?), your use of physical contact (Do you physically interact; why or why not?), and your sense of time (Do you feel rushed/impatient or distracted?). Does your physical presence communicate: "I really want to be here"? You will create a particular atmosphere by the kind of style you choose: celebration, explanation, dialogue, or lecture. As a result the children will perceive the sermon as "their time," "your time," or "our time"; they will sense whether you are preaching or teaching *at* them or sharing *with* them. Remember, you are creating a total experience and the details add up.

Tone is important whenever we communicate, but it is even more important when we communicate with children, for they are intuitive observers of the unconscious and the unspoken. The content of a specific sermon may prove to be irrelevant or over their heads, but children always pick up on the tone of the message. Since younger children are less confident about their use of language, they give more weight to nonlinguistic clues. This factor can work both to our advantage and our disadvantage. On the one hand, we need not despair if children feel left out of a particular experience; the tone of a sermon can succeed when the content fails. The sermon "Baa-Baa" tells the story of the concern of a certain shepherd who searches for the one who has gotten lost. As it unfolds the story relies upon an allegory of a lamb named Baa-Baa (the child) and the good shepherd (God) who leaves the flock (safe and sound in their pen) to find the lost lamb. Before I told the story I did not presume the younger children would "catch" the analogy. But I did intend for them to be touched by the tone of the story — how it is told — and the shepherd's caring and the lamb's great worth. So at one level the sermon missed the mark, but on a tonal plane it succeeded. A similar example is the sermon "Death Comes To The Henry Family," because some of its concepts about life and death are too abstract for younger minds. Nevertheless, the emotive qualities of assurance and anticipation can be translated into verbal and nonverbal clues that children can experience.

Anyone familiar with the work of Jerome Berryman is sensitized to the importance of setting, tone, and tactile clues. Berryman provides detailed suggestions about how the teaching room is to be organized, how the teacher walks and speaks, the level at which the interaction happens. His intention is that children will experience God in mystery, awe, and wonderment in how we present ourselves. Berryman emphasizes teaching with space and time, or the rhythm of church school time, and together these become "the unspoken lesson." One other key component to Berryman's methodology is "the response of wondering together." In contrast to a question-answer format, the children first share a common experience (the story telling) and then are asked "to bring their own experiences into dialogue with the biblical stories ... so the children themselves have a way of making meaning and order in their lives" (*Young Children and Worship*, pp. 14-15). After the story of the

Good Shepherd, the children might be asked, "I wonder how it feels to be lost," or "I wonder how the Good Shepherd feels about the sheep," or "I wonder who the Good Shepherd might really be." I highly commend what Berryman has achieved, for it is the one truly innovative approach to teaching/proclaiming in a long time. It certainly made me more aware of the physical environment, my movements, the rate of my speech, the use of nonverbal clues in order to affect a specific purpose. Wonderment and mystery are woefully neglected in children's sermons. This is particularly curious when gospel-telling takes place in the larger context of worship and the sanctuary.

Targeting Your Sermon

On most Sundays the minister sees before him a group of children ranging from toddlers to adolescents. Ideally, she would like to have a small group of preschoolers or third and fourth graders. But since the ideal is usually impossible, the minister should at least be aware of some basic differences in how children of different ages perceive and verbalize reality. As a general rule, the pastor should aim his sermon at the lowest common denominator, which would normally be first and second grades. Because it takes more effort to enter into a child's world, ministers too often address the older children because they are closer to their mental and verbal abilities. The negative result is an adult sermon reduced to pint size.

This business of focusing a children's message is not as difficult as it seems. A basic understanding of the developmental stages of children will go a long way. I make a threefold division: preschool, younger children, older children. Junior and Senior High are unique categories. There are, of course, more definitive classifications of development. Lawrence Kohlberg, for example, has identified six stages occurring at three distinct levels: pre-conventional, conventional, and post-conventional. Just a little time spent reading Kohlberg's theory of moral development (*Moral Development: A Guide to Piaget and Kohlberg* by Ronald Duska and Mariellen Whelan) or Margaret Donaldson's *Children's Minds* will deepen anyone's appreciation for the very distinct stages of development.[6]

Preschoolers. The most important generalization about preschoolers is their inability to understand abstractions or to make analogical connections. Words are not so much a symbol of some reality as a coequal representation of some specific reality. Attributes like "good," "red," "strong," "big" are embodied in the person or object itself. "Dog" is Spot down the street rather than all animals in the world with certain characteristics. Preschoolers may come to understand the cross as the thing on which Jesus died, but they will not grasp the Cross as a symbol of Christ's atonement for humanity. Consequently, teachers of the Word should watch their use of metaphors, allegories, complex stories. On the other hand, children of this age love role-playing, let's-pretend games, rhymes, and stories that are not allegorical (see, for example, "Stilling The Storm" vs. "Devils Are For Sale, Aren't They?").

The second generalization is that preschoolers think literally. They also do not distinguish well between fact and fantasy. Consequently, preschoolers will draw unusual conclusions from what they hear and see. The first time I told the story "Looking For The Devil" my daughter alerted me to the need to watch my language. In trying to tell why the Devil is not really a red character with a pitchfork whom we can blame for the bad things we do, I had innocently said, "The Devil is inside of you." Several weeks later my four-year-old asked me one night at supper, "Daddy, is there a Devil in my stomach?" By a process of literal association, she had come to the simple conclusion that if the Devil doesn't live somewhere outside, then "he" must live inside her, and where else but in her stomach — a conclusion made "logical" by the fact that she had a stomachache. It is this predisposition toward literalism that explains why preschoolers invariably misconstrue analogies, although ministers persist in using them. New Testament scholarship may have relieved us of this burden (if it is a burden of obligation rather than laziness) by demonstrating that most or all allegories were originally parables of participation which the Church turned into parables of illustration (see "The Story Form As Proclamation").

One reason preschoolers are so much fun to be with is their ability to move easily between a literal world and a world of fantasy. We love to read to them because of all the wonderful, zany books that titillate the imagination. So go ahead and try a few let's pretend gospel messages. Admit to your hesitation of associating the Bible with make believe. At the same time indulge the child who visits other worlds, the worlds C. S. Lewis created for the benefit of adults and children. Think of fantasy not so much as fiction or escapism but as a doorway into a world where dreams arise, fears are discharged, and all things are possible. Preschoolers will love it and love you if you will enter this world with them.

As adults we may find it strange that children do not share our fear of death — so strange that we continually try to protect them from seeing the signs of death. How quickly we forget that children do not see the world of angels and the world of decay as two irreconcilable realities. On the one side, they are remarkably down-to-earth (Who will tuck me in bed if Mommy has gone to be with God?). In their minds fact and fantasy are likely to be interchangeable, which explains why miracles and magic are neither puzzling nor awe-inspiring to preschoolers. One of the sermons in this collection, "Stilling The Storm," gives children the opportunity to sense and feel what it is like to be in a small boat in a big sea. Older children may be reluctant to participate because they have "adult" reasons not to believe they have an oar in their hands. It is too bad that the adult in us keeps us from this kind of "teleportation."

Younger or Elementary Children. After children enter school they change markedly. Among the most important changes is their need to demonstrate both to themselves and to their peers and parents that they belong and that they are capable of being independent. By age eight or nine their center of gravity begins to shift from home to school. Parents are often distressed by what their child is learning when away from home: from friends and peer groups, television, and from overhearing adults. The pastor is readily associated with those authorities from which the child is trying to separate and as a result is sensitive to preaching that is morally righteous and heard as "do this" and "don't do that." The virtue of being different because one is a Christian is heard as an invitation to be seen as different and thus standing alone. By far the most realistic situations are ones where elementary school children are conscious of peer interaction (see "What To Do With A Chocolate Chip Cookie?"), where children of the same age act out their real-life tensions (see "Show Me How Strong You Are"). The most effective communication flows in and through the group, in contrast to communication which is directed at them and flows from the minister/teacher to them.

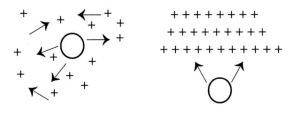

Older Children. The older child (grades 4, 5, and 6) intensifies the traits of younger children but is more interested in mastering and controlling reality. After school activities are less play and more testing, getting ahead, and finding oneself. Peer pressure becomes more intense. Both boys and girls are able and eager to distinguish clearly between reality and fantasy. Video games, television, and movies are more than escapism; they are ways of "acting out" and projecting who they might be. Magic becomes intriguing because just as they have figured out some basic rules about the universe, someone comes along and seems to defy them. At the same time they are less interested in the world of make-believe and more likely to identify with the "real" people of MTV and sports. "Let's pretend" now seems childish but role-playing is still acceptable if the roles are realistic. In fact, role playing can be very valuable, since it provides older children the opportunity to experiment with what it will be like to be older.

Children have a limited perception of time and the teacher in each of us becomes frustrated when children make Moses and Jesus contemporaries. We must continually remind ourselves that for preschoolers time is nothing more than a patchwork of uncoordinated events. Even during the middle years of childhood, time is limited to the narrow span between the birth of a baby brother and the death of Grandma. It is only in early adolescence that they can put into perspective 2,000 years of biblical history and 2,000 years of church history. Thus, we might as well wait until junior high or high school to separate the prophet Isaiah from the Apostle Paul and concentrate instead on what a prophet or a disciple does.

Watching Your Language

No matter what the age group, watch your language. Take nothing for granted. A simple explanation of a key word is one way of getting into your theme. (See "A Prince In Disguise," where the word "disguise" is first explained.) Children do not live in a biblical world and therefore have a limited understanding of words like "reconciliation," "righteousness," "repentance," "salvation," "covenant," "shepherd," "disciple," "grace," "sin," and "holy." Consider for a moment the story of the Good Samaritan. The meaning of this story depends upon an understanding of who a Samaritan was in the eyes of those who passed by on the other side. I am still struggling with a suitable parallel. "A person with AIDS" once worked very well and avoided a lengthy explanation of Samaritan. Sometimes the listener needs to be prepared for the telling of a story in order for the experience to be recreated. Everything may hinge upon the meaning of a single word. Occasionally there are sermons that require us to prepare the setting, as would be the case in any of the biblical stories regarding a leper. Otherwise, the gospel of God's grace and inclusion is not an experience but a lesson to be heard and forgotten.

Most of us know of at least one humorous story about a child who misunderstood a word and came up with a preposterous interpretation. I once referred to Jesus as being of the house and lineage of David. Then realizing they didn't have a clue of what was meant, I added that Jesus was a descendent of King David. Later, a girl approached me hesitantly and said as politely as she could, "Mr. Coleman, I'm sure glad Jesus descended from David and not into Hell." Often we unwittingly choose words that reflect a dualism that we do not intend; for example, we may casually

49

refer to "God up there" or "the Devil down there." Since children learn as much, if not more, from our mistakes as from our good intentions, we must be on guard — particularly of the more insidious forms of dualism inviting children to picture God as up in heaven (wherever that is) and therefore could not possibly have anything to do with what happens on the school playground. We undermine the Christian faith when we use a distinct biblical language to convey what was originally proclaimed in the vernacular. Rather than talking about sin as a doctrine or a concept, why not talk about sin as children experience it? If we inherently have difficulty associating sin with children, then we need to remember that "overreaching" is a human characteristic which develops in tandem with the maturation of the ego. I have yet to meet a child who knows what it means when told that Jesus died for your sins. What does the Cross have to do with the unmerciful teasing of my brother, a child wonders? More than 2,000 years separate American culture from a Jewish Messiah, and repeating the well-worn phrases will not build any bridges. We need to forgo attempting to translate those lofty doctrines and symbols we finally understand after a college degree and several years of theological training. If, instead, we utilize those common experiences that bind all humans together, we will discover that we do indeed speak the same language.

An effective way to rethink the language you use is to ask children to draw a picture of God and another picture of God doing something. This may be an appraisal of their entire church-life experience, since they are learning stories, absorbing sights and sounds, and fashioning mental images from everyone and everything they encounter. The story of the talents in Matthew 25 is a reminder that Jesus paid more than scant attention to correcting the wrong image of God (in this instance the critical, demanding, unforgiving depiction of God; see the question mark at the end of v. 26). Yours will be the uncommon congregation if the children (and adults) draw pictures of God, Jesus, or the Holy Spirit in the midst of their daily lives.

Heart, Mind, And Spirit

There is a holism in being human and there is a holism in the gospel to be proclaimed. We are told to love God with all our heart, mind, and soul (Deuteronomy 6:5; Matthew 22:37). Jesus, we are told, grew in wisdom (mind), stature (body), and favor with God (spirit). Therefore, let there be a holism in what we proclaim to children. One message will speak more to the mind, another more to the body, and another more to the spirit.

For some reason the YMCA's logo — △ — made an early impression on me. It was important to me, and still is, that I nurture my body, mind, and soul. I also learned the "Y" was better equipped to help me grow in body, the school in mind, and the church in spirit, but that is not to say these institutions did not value all three dimensions of being human. We who labor within the church and for the sake of the gospel should, nevertheless, seek "God's kingdom and righteousness" above all (Matthew 6:33). But that does not mean there is never a gospel word for the body or the mind. The Jesus of the New Testament takes almost no notice of such distinctions. He encounters each person at his or her deepest need: the woman with the flow of blood of forty years, the inquiring Nicodemus, the young man asking what he must do to have eternal life. It wasn't usually the Good News they expected or wanted to hear, and that is the way it is with the Word that transforms.

Children are growing. That is, they are unceasingly changing and becoming. This can both drive us crazy and energize us. We see in them an unbridled enthusiasm for the world God made, an almost naive willingness to love others, and a love of God that emanates from "one fresh from God." We are called to be a part of whom they will *become*. In no small measure they will become what they see in our hearts, hear from our lips, observe in our actions. When all is said and done what matters most is how we live the gospel in our bodies, and in our hearts, and in our souls.

Music

It is not necessary to extol the power of music, especially in the lives of the young, or defend sacred music as a legitimate expression of the Christian faith. Music appears to be hard-wired into the soul of every human being, though it can be damped by cultural influences. It has a certain simplicity and directness that verbal communication often lacks. When the words are simple and the tune is catchy, songs have a staying power that rival stories. Beginning with the premise that music is a powerful way to convey the gospel, the question is how and to what end.

To what end? Most congregations have some type of musical program for children and/or youth. The children's or youth choir is typical; the purpose is to provide an occasional anthem. Everyone loves to see and hear them standing in front and are anxious to let them know, usually with applause, that they are appreciated and valued. It is time to take a more critical theological look at what is going on. When their role is to provide a musical selection (anthem), then what is the purpose of the anthem in a specific worship context? The drift toward entertainment is always present and in spite of our resistance the pull is considerable. The larger question concerns the role of the choir regardless of the age of the participants. The cardinal rule is this: sacred music inspires (uplifts) the soul, teaches the heart to love the triune God, and can be a religious experience in and of itself. In short, sacred music embodies the gospel. The role of the choir, then, is to help lead worship by inspiring, consoling, welcoming, sending, teaching, proclaiming, and above all else, glorifying God.

To achieve this end, *preparation* is the necessary ingredient. To prepare a children's anthem, perform it, and move on to the next occasion is to short circuit the very purpose of sacred music. Good preparation includes the right attitude, a clear sense of purpose, a feel for the rhythm, an understanding of the content. When children sing or dance or play musical instruments within worship, they become worship leaders. What specifically is their purpose and how they lead worship on a particular Sunday depends upon the selection and where it is placed. It is common sense to appreciate that a solemn selection requires a different preparation from a joyful (bordering perhaps on silly) piece. Yes, the sacred can be silly when it incites a smile or causes a hint of self-recognition. When music and children are the medium, you have a combination that is potent. How can we not thank God for child-like innocence,

52

boundless energy, exuberant joyfulness, and songful voices to tell the Good News?

How? The possibilities are great. Different congregations are trying rhythm or percussion instruments (also known as Orff named after a particular kind of rhythm instrument), wind ensembles, Kazoo "bands," as well as hand bells and choral groups. A number of excellent how-to resources are available, such as *Children Sing His Praise: A Handbook for Children's Choir Directors* (edited by Donald Rotermund). A better effort can be made toward integrating children, youth, and adults so they are not heard as separate choirs but reflective voices of the entire congregation. There are pieces written with this kind of incorporation in mind.[7] Otherwise, a little creativity (original arrangements) goes a long way.[8] For those who direct and teach children and youth, the mechanics should not be allowed to override the sense of being called to a ministry of music. It is wonderful how using the right words, such as "ministry," can change the child's perspective and empower him or her to sing for God.

What Should Children Sing — traditional vs. popular? My response is both, and the question becomes how to accomplish this. How does one find time to teach both traditional hymnody and music that is specifically written for children. This correctly implies that traditional hymns were not written with children in mind. The reason we do not neglect this particular style of music, or wait until they have become adults, is to *begin* the connection with the apostolic Church (the church that endures what is popular). The classic hymns convey a sense of Church that is bigger, older, and universal ("one Holy Catholic and Apostolic Church"). For this reason alone there is value for children to be present when hymns are sung well and with enthusiasm. But this experience can be greatly enhanced with a modicum of planning. When children gather for rehearsal, the hymn for the coming Sunday can be introduced. The children's anthem can be a hymn. Before the worship service begins (along with the announcements if they are placed here) children can be introduced to the hymn (while adults "listen in"). *We do our children a great disservice and teach them they are not valued when they are present for worship and all of the music is "not for them."* When the first hymn is being selected, keep the children in mind. With a little imagination the first hymn can be played and sung so it achieves its purpose of adoration for the *entire* congregation. Utilizing your critical eye, look about for other places in worship where music is being thrown away, for example, the music when children exit for their classes or the music when they enter for communion. If in fact it is traveling music, then it should be a song they can sing and enjoy singing. If it is a communion hymn or song, then the children should know it (learn it) and participate as do the adults in preparation for receiving the Lord's Supper.

By popular sacred music I am referring to the wide selection of music that is contemporary (in sync with the language and mindset of the participants). The lyrics and music are more accessible and informal. Whether traditional or popular, further consideration should be given to make the "anthem" be the children's sermon. Rather than having it stand alone, begin with an introduction, discuss it after it is sung, involve the entire congregation. In other words, let the anthem be an experience of the sacred, a proclamation of the gospel!

For those congregations that have a separate family worship service, or are planning to initiate one, I urge you to make music a core experience. Here you have the time and the latitude to teach and prepare so the singing and the clapping, the dancing and the playing, are meaningful. Greater attention can be given to age appropriateness — what strikes the chord for a four-year-old will not resonate with a fourteen-year-old. Remember, *variety* is also the spice for effective gospel-telling when the medium is music.

The Story Form As Proclamation

Using Storytelling In Gospel-Telling

There has been considerable interest in the preacher as story-teller and the gospel as God's story.[9] Biblical studies have strengthened the perception that the Bible is not only a book of stories but uses the narrative as a distinctive way of proclaiming the Good News in Jesus Christ. Storytelling and gospel-telling, then, are inextricably bound together. Frederick Buechner points out that the preacher needs to tell only two stories — his own and God's — and demonstrate where the two intersect.[10]

The story form seems a natural for children's sermons, not only because it is biblical but because children enjoy a good story. But we shouldn't embrace the art of storytelling without considerable clarification and qualification. We must remember that stories are a natural repository of metaphors, analogies, symbolic representation, and indirection — all of which pose particular problems for younger children. The story form is both alluring and allusive, stimulating and confusing, fascinating and confounding. In short, it is a powerful tool of communication but it can be delusive in the wrong hands. Amos Wilder aptly states the unique feature of the story form in its purest sense.

> *Now we know that a true metaphor or symbol is more than a sign, it is a bearer of reality to which it refers. The hearer not only learns about the reality, he participates in it. He is invaded by it. Here lies the power and fatefulness of art. Jesus' speech had the character not of instruction and ideas but of compelling imagination, of spell and mythical shock and transformation. Not just in an aesthetic sense but in the service of the Gospel.* — *Early Christian Rhetoric*, p. 84

Like Jesus' parables, a story draws in its listeners and lets us participate in the action, almost without our knowing it. This is a story's alluring quality, and the benefits are considerable. "A large part of the power of the parable," writes John Shea, "is that you do not see it coming. Parable is blind-side storytelling" (*Stories of God*, p. 182). Unlike a moralistic story, which has a maxim that the listener anticipates long before it comes, the parabolic story teaches by indirection. The classic biblical example is Nathan's indirect indictment of David by way of a parable (2 Samuel 12). Because Nathan fears for his life, knowing that King David is known for his angry outbursts, he wisely avoids a direct confrontation (telling it like it is). But the mode of communication he chooses is effective, because David indicted himself in overhearing a story he thought was about someone else.

Overhearing The Gospel

According to Fred Craddock, distance and participation are the two basic factors involved in "overhearing the gospel."[11] Because the gospel upsets all conventional wisdom and challenges us to be more than we presently are, we are ambivalent about hearing what God wants to say to us. We would prefer to "listen in" at a safe distance so that we can beat a hasty retreat if necessary. In fact, we have always needed distance to deal with our unspoken fears. Children, for example, love ghost stories because they are real enough to voice their inner fears but not so real that their spell cannot be broken by hiding under the covers or turning on a light. Experience also teaches us that adults are most attentive when "listening in" on a children's story. Is a child ever more attentive than when overhearing an adult (i.e. forbidden) conversation behind a closed door or sitting on the stairwell? For the very same reason it is tempting to speak to adults while they overhear the gospel-telling. In both instances listeners tune in because they can participate at a safe distance — which is the psychology behind good storytelling. As a masterful storyteller, Jesus utilized the methodology of "overhearing the gospel" to its fullest potential when he told parables. The power of the parable lies precisely in its ability to convince the hearer that he is overhearing someone else's story. Consequently, he lowers his defenses and is drawn into the story, discovering, then or later, that he is the one the story is about. In the parable addressed to "one who was trying to justify himself," does he have any idea that this story of a Samaritan would have anything to do with himself? Or was he blind-sided when this irredeemable outcast of a Samaritan turns out to be the super hero worthy of imitation?

Every good storyteller knows that she is most effective when she does not have to spell out the meaning of her story; for the story itself carries its message best when the listener finds her own story within the one that is being told. The Bible is the unparalleled example of how each generation retells the story of a previous generation in such a way that it discovers anew its own identity.[12] Essential in this process of overhearing and participation is an "empty space" which enables the listener to "work on" the story for herself. This characteristic of the parable-story is enhanced by its *open-ended* nature. Bruno Bettelheim, the noted psychiatrist, claims the relevance of the fairy tale lies in its open-ended character: "The fairy tale is therapeutic because the patient listener finds his own solutions through contemplating what the story seems to imply about him and his inner conflicts at this moment in his life."[13] Bettelheim then proceeds to show by carefully analyzing several classic fairy tales that while some have a fixed conclusion (a happy ending), all have suggestive details that invite the listener to identify with the characters, and all pose many questions to be answered. Why, for example, does the "innocent" Red Riding Hood (a virgin dressed in red) disobey her mother and stray from the path and meet up with the predatorial wolf? The story raises the question but never answers it. Thus the fairy tale is distinctive because, unlike fables and moralistic stories, it teaches by encouraging the listener/participant to explore what might happen if she disobeys the rules and acts upon her fantasies or fears. While some stories will end with a satisfying conclusion, other stories will never end because they are open-ended. If this discussion convinces you of anything, it should throw a critical light on the inclination to explain and over explain and even to question whether the primary purpose of gospel-telling is to explain anything.

This handbook offers several stories and demonstrations that are purposefully left unfinished, because they are meant to be discussed, extended, and worked on whenever the Spirit moves (e.g.,

"Yesterday I Stomped On A Frog" and "Sammy No Share"). The principle of overhearing also allows us to work on more than one layer of meaning at the same time. As you target your children's sermon, you know others will be listening in. While they are not the primary participants, a super-good gospel-telling will have enough "spill over" meaning to draw others in. D. B. Johnson's book, *Henry Builds a Cabin*, is a delightful children's book about a bear who builds a modest cabin ("It's bigger than it looks"). At a later stage of development the same child, when studying the life of Henry David Thoreau, could have an "aha" experience: I remember a story about a bear who built a cabin in the woods by a pond. The sermon, "My One-tenth Box," begins with a child-like understanding of Christian stewardship, but it has tentacles reaching into a broader, more mature understanding of Christian stewardship. On a subtler level, "Breakfast Of Champions" opens a can of worms for youth and adults as they come to grips with unfulfilled dreams, priorities, and achieving a balance between competing values and priorities.

Becoming A Good Storyteller

Can there be any doubt that a well-formulated story is ideally suited to convey the Good News to children? It works not so much because it conveys new content or holds up an exemplary model, but because it allows for self-recognition. John Dominic Crossan explains the challenge facing us when we try to become good storytellers.

> *It is one thing to communicate to others' conclusions and admonitions based upon one's own profound spiritual experience. It was this that Pharisaic theology did so admirably at the time of Jesus. It is quite another thing to try and communicate that experience itself, or, better, to assist people to find their own ultimate encounter. This is what Jesus' parables seek to do: to help others into their own experience of the Kingdom and to draw from that experience their own way of life.*
> — In Parables, p. 52

This quotation recalls the distinction between the indicative and the imperative. Stories that aim to convey a moral imperative are usually closed and direct. Stories that hope the listener will experience the love of God are usually open-ended and indirect. Two superb examples of the former are Aesop's Fables and the stories of Hans Christian Anderson. Stories modeled after Aesop's fables have two things to teach us. They are short and so easily remembered that they have staying power. Second, children like repetition; a story that has an essence that can be captured in a simple phrase makes it extremely portable ("If you 'crow' about yourself, you may regret it" from the fable, "The Fox and the Crow."[14]) Anderson's "The Ugly Duckling" and "The Emperor's New Clothes" are consummate examples of stories that beg for a Christian adaptation. Our public libraries are filled with delightful children's books, and when at a loss for an idea, we often turn to these. The question we need to ask ourselves is, "Do they work? That is, do they convey the gospel?"

As a partial answer consider the types of stories at our disposal:
secular,
biblical,
biographical (e.g., Saint Francis of Assisi), and
autobiographical.

Jerry Jordan in his "Brown Bag" series of children sermons often builds his message around a personal experience which is then given a Christian interpretation; or we might say he tells a personal story in order to make the gospel real and personal. They are effective because they are direct, the language is level, and the message is embodied in the messenger. Jerome Berryman tells biblical stories but what makes his approach so different is how he concludes. Rather than closing off the story, he leaves it open-ended by asking a series of "I wonder" questions. In the story of "Jesus is Risen: The Road to Emmaus," the storyteller ends by asking: "I wonder how Jesus' friends felt when Jesus died." "I wonder what it felt like to recognize Jesus in the breaking of the bread." "I wonder what it was like to tell others that Jesus is alive." Note, the questions come after the children and minister have shared a common experience (the story) and that the questions do not have a definitive answer. They are meant to keep the conversation going.

So, to answer the question about which stories are appropriate, my response is that it depends. Regardless of the source of the story, in our telling of it the gospel must be heard. Second, a decision is required concerning its form: biographical, autobiographical, fictional in the sense that you created it, direct and level, or multi-level and open-ended. The most important question is whether feelings have been sufficiently stirred (brought to the surface) so that a space has been made for Jesus to enter in.

The Ten Commandments
Of Gospel-Telling

1. Make it your aim for each sermon to leave an impression rather than to make a point.

2. Always include the day-to-day experiences of the children you are addressing.

3. Be aware of biblical stories originally meant for adults. Be conscious of the literal interpretation that younger children will attach to almost everything you say.

4. Do not teach children anything that they will need to relearn later.

5. Do not read anything unless it is a personal letter. Instead, tell the Story in such a way that children experience God's love as radical reversal and surprising joy.

6. Place each children's sermon within a context: (a) within the service of worship which develops a central theme; (b) within the curriculum of the church school; (c) within a broader context which includes developing sound Christian images useful in the process of becoming a disciple.

7. Remember that sermons with the greatest impact are those which actively and physically involve the listener; and that what is seen and heard are second best. Keep in mind the learning pyramid and that what we experience is what we keep.

8. Know the basic differences among preschool, younger, and older children. Then decide how best to target your sermon with "spill over" for others.

9. Watch your language. Keep in mind that although similes and allegories may be clear to you, they will probably confuse children.

10. Ask yourself two questions: Am I trivializing the gospel by focusing on character-building (moralism) or by offering a pearl of wisdom (humanism)? Am I neglecting the One who empowers us to overcome hate with love?

Part II

Variety: The Spice Of Gospel-Telling

The following definitions and classifications
provide the rationale for how sermons are organized and review some of the distinctions
made in Part I.

Definitions

Let's Pretend — A sermon which requires listeners to use their imagination in a vivid way. The sermon "Sammy No Share" utilizes an imaginary person. While no description is given of how he looks, it is a good idea to take the time to paint a picture with details. "Death Comes To The Henry Family" utilizes flannel graph figures. While they are tangible they become imaginary figures as listeners translate mother and father and siblings into their own situation. The reason for the cutout figures is to help identify each person as they speak. Using a different voice, if done well, might be sufficient but it seemed like a stretch to me. Let's Pretend sermons bring out the actor in each of us.

Visual Demonstrations — A sermon in which an object is intrinsic to the message. There are many dimensions for an object to be used. It can be a starting point, an illustration, a reminder by association, a simile (the object is like something else). In its most widely understood sense, an object lesson is a lesson arising from an object. Having someone turn the lights in the church off and on in order to throw light upon (illustrate) Jesus' saying that he is the Light of the world is an object lesson. The lesson in this instance would be that Jesus is like a light because he helps us to see things clearly and not to get lost in the darkness of sin. The breaking of an egg in the sermon "Humpty Dumpty Had A Great Fall" is interesting for several reasons. It is a visual demonstration of death. It does involve an analogy (death is like the breaking of an egg). What makes it different from the light switch is its dramatic impact (how often do we see an egg dropped in church?) and its lower level of abstraction (death is pictured as an irreversible process). The same is true for the sermon "God Doesn't Make Telephone Calls" where the telephone is intrinsic to the opposing experience of speaking with God heart-to-heart. In other words, not all objects are the same.

Dramatic Participation — A sermon given in the spirit of the parable requiring the listener's actual participation in the drama. There are degrees and a variety of participation. Eating an apple activates all our senses. Ringing a bell and making a promise is making a decision marked with a dramatic action. Participation, when compared to listening, is a worthy goal since it creates an experience, and experiences have a certain "staying power."

Pantomime and Echo — The pantomime is intriguing because our outer sense of hearing is turned off and as a result the inner voice is turned on. The inner voice — the voice of the conscience or the ulterior ego — sets up the conversation when making an ethical decision. Pantomime also activates the imagination and once activated is easily "called up" again. Echo sermons — a favorite with children — are potent because they utilize participation and repetition. And they are fun.

The Story — A sermon with a well-defined plot and characters (and therefore not an anecdote). A story is always best told. When you read from a storybook, do so because of the illustrations. Before you tell or read, clarify for yourself what is the gospel message you are communicating. Keep in mind the diversity of forms: biography, autobiography, fictional, biblical, family/ancestral, fable. Remember the value of keeping the story open-ended so the listener can work on the story when the time is right. The best gospel-telling stories are those about identity: whom we identify with, finding our identity through the living experiences of another, reclaiming our identity.

Parable — This is not a form I have attempted and therefore no examples are provided. The spirit of the parable, though, is alive in much of what I do. A parable can function as a simile by illustrating the redemptive process. But when they function as metaphor, the parables of Jesus are powerful stories which *reverse* our natural attitudes and actions. As an illustrative story one can listen and walk away, but as a parable-story you are drawn in, often by overhearing, only to realize a decision is required of you.

Parables turn our known world upside down. Both John Shea and Walter Brueggemann (see bibliography) are excellent teachers of the parabolic methodology as utilized by the prophets and Jesus.

The Prophets — This is not a specific form. These sermons are included to exemplify the meaning of "prophetic" in both biblical and contemporary settings. They are meant to encourage a "speaking forth" about justice and mercy to the nation, the church, and individuals.

Let's Pretend

These sermons require the listeners to use
their imaginations in a vivid way.

Death Comes To The Henry Family

Text: John 14:1ff.

Season: Any

Summary: Through death, we enter God's eternal Kingdom. (Children have the capacity to understand this basic Christian message.)

Props: Flannel-graph and figures: Mother and Father (I prefer Mother and Father grouped as one, representing the parental figure; this also makes the role easier to play and more adaptable for single-parent families); Judy (in junior high), Michael (six years old), and Sharon (four years old). Figures can be cut from a magazine and backed with felt or masking tape.

Preparation: Begin by introducing each person and giving his or her age.

Scene I

(Mother, Father, and Judy)

Mother: We sure will miss Grandma around here.

Father: Yes, we will. We knew she was sick and might die soon, but just the same, I wish she could have lived a few more years. What's bothering me is *what* we should tell Michael and Sharon.

Mother: I think we should wait to tell them. You know how the children loved their grandmother.

Judy: I think we should tell them now — they have a right to know.

Mother: You're right, of course, but I don't know if they'll understand what has happened.

Father: Does it really matter if they understand everything? They'll understand enough in their own way.

Scene II

(Add Michael and Sharon)

Michael and Sharon: We heard. We heard you and Mommy talking. Did Grandma really die?

Father: Yes, she did. She died last night.

Michael: Does that mean we'll never see her again? Has she gone away to see God?

Sharon: I want to see Grandma. I want to see her now.

Mother: We can't see her, Sharon. It's going to be hard but we'll have to learn to live our lives without Grandma from now on.

Sharon: I don't care. I want to be with her.

Father: I know it isn't easy for you to understand, but Grandma has gone to a different world — a world you've never seen before, but a world where you can be very, very close to God.

Judy: I never thought of it like that before, but death is like a bridge.* The only way we can cross over to God's world is by passing over the bridge of death.

Michael: I wish I could see what God's Kingdom is like.

Mother: Someday I know you will, but for the moment you'll have to enjoy God's Kingdom as it is here on earth.

71

Judy: Does God have two Kingdoms?

Mother: No, Judy. I didn't mean to confuse everyone. When Jesus came to earth he started a Kingdom based upon love — one that includes our world and Grandma's world. You might even say that we are trying to help God complete that Kingdom every time we love instead of hate.

Judy: But Grandma doesn't have to wait any longer, does she? She's already there.

Father: I guess you could put it that way. Grandma is now able to love God with all her heart and mind and spirit.

Michael: I know Grandma won't be able to take us on any more trips, but I'm glad she crossed over that bridge to be closer to God.

Father: The Bible doesn't answer all of our questions about death, but it does promise the most important thing. Death is the end of one journey, but it is also the beginning of a new one. God showed us that when Jesus was raised from the dead. We'll be sad that Grandma is gone, but thankful that God will give Grandma a new life in a world where love is everywhere.

Reflection Note: The power of this type of sermon comes from the situation itself: the children are allowed to listen in as another family talks about a very sensitive subject (see Part I, "The Story Form As Proclamation").

---

*Throughout the conversation I have avoided using language that implies that death is like sleep or that God's eternal Kingdom is a place with a specific location. Both analogies are unbiblical and teach children concepts which they must relearn later. Listen to other people's discussions of death, and you will discover how common these two notions are.

Sammy No Share

Text: Romans 12:21

Season: UNICEF/Halloween or any occasion when children are being asked to share with others.

Summary: The Gospel is not only about sharing with others who have less but also sharing with those who have much but do not know how to share.

Props: Apple, toy, candy

Note: Younger children often have an imaginary playmate and most of us have a shadow self. As an imaginary figure, Sammy No Share may appear any place, any time.

This morning I would like you to meet a "friend" (*hesitate before saying "friend" because Sammy No Share is not quite a friend*) of mine. (*Look to your right and wait for him to "materialize," then put your arm around him.*) This is Sammy No Share. I know you are saying that you can't see him, but believe me, Sammy No Share is everywhere, and right now he is here. If you are having difficulty seeing Sammy No Share, this story will help. And since we can't see Sammy No Share, I will be his hands and mouth.

Let me tell you — Sammy is all hands and mouth. (*Place on the floor an apple, two or three pieces of candy, a toy, and so forth. Take the apple and say, assuming a different posture for Sammy.*) Yummy, I love apples — cold, crisp apples that fill your mouth with such a sweet crunch. I could share with you but I think not. After all, my name is Sammy No Share. And here is a _____ (*name a toy*) that I am not going to share with you. If you think I am going to let you play with it, think again. Ah, some candy. (*Open one piece and eat it.*) Yummy, that was good. And I've got two pieces left. I think I'll put these in my pocket for later. (*Gather*

73

up the toy and the apple.) Well, I think I'm off. See you later. Oh, I know you think I should have shared with you, but there is a reason they call me Sammy No Share.

(*Pause for the children to digest what they heard and saw.*) Well, there you have it. Sammy No Share. I'm just as glad he is gone. I wonder what we could do to change Sammy? (*Entertain ideas.*)

Reflection Note: One possibility is to leave the gospel-telling open-ended until next Sunday and then incorporate one or more of the suggestions. Repeat the opening. Hopefully you will have the same suggestion I did: As we share our toys and goodies with Sammy he would learn how to share. I ended the gospel-telling with changing Sammy's name to Sammy Share A Lot. The emphasis is not so much about sharing but how to change someone who won't share.

I feel a prayer coming on. Join me please. "Gracious God, we have so much to share with others and we know you do not want us to be like Sammy No Share. And while it won't be easy, with your help, we could show others what a good feeling it is when we share a lot. Amen."

Show Me How Strong You Are

Text: Matthew 5:38-42; Luke 23:34

Season: Lent, any time

Summary: The stronger you are, the more you can love someone who is hating you. This is a sermon more suitable for older
children.

Preparation: Divide the children into two groups with an equal
number of boys and girls in each group. Explain that this is a Let's
Pretend game and that it is a game about how we judge who is the
strongest. Ask the groups to face each other (*you can begin with
having them seated with a spokesperson/s standing up*). Ask one
group to pretend they are playground bullies. Have them assume a
posture of toughness and meanness toward the other group. Let
them gesture some threatening words. Ask the other group to stand
up. Ask them what they are going to do about these threats. Ask
them all to sit down again as two groups confronting each other.

Ask the groups to continue Let's Pretend. What would group
A do if they heard group B has knives? If one group has a powerful laser gun? The other group has missiles armed with atomic
warheads? Going further, let's pretend this nation over here has
just fired a missile on one of your cities. And if they did this, are
you going to stand by and take that?

You remember, we began with a seemingly innocent playground fight and now we have a war. Jesus said he understood
how we have learned to act that way: an eye for an eye and a tooth
for a tooth. So I ask you, how do we change the way we and everyone else act? Begin to guide the discussion toward the question of
who is the stronger person or nation: the one who begins a fight or
the one who finds a way not to return blow for blow.

We might not think of Jesus as the strongest person in the
world, because we associate strength with fists and armies and fire

power. Aren't we the strongest nation in the world because we have the best weapons of destruction? Because Jesus knew very well how it is with the world, he decided to give us an example of how to change the way we act when someone is out to hurt us or hate us. He knew he had to do more than just tell us to return love for hate until love overcomes hate. So Jesus, when they had nailed him to a cross to die, looked out and said, "Father-God, forgive them, for they know not what they are doing."

You will have to decide for yourself whether Jesus is the strongest person in the world and what it means to be the strongest nation in the world. I can truthfully say that the world is waiting for your answer!

Reflection Note: This sermon ends by inviting a response which the children must complete in their own time and in their own way. This type of sermon should not be turned into a moralistic teaching but left open-ended. The inviting itself is a characteristic of good storytelling and Jesus' parables.

Stilling The Storm

Text: Matthew 8:23-27

Season: Any

Summary: Like the disciples, we must learn to trust the Lord.

Props: A cushion

Preparation: Begin by showing the children a picture of Jesus stilling the storm or another picture depicting a storm in its full fury.

This morning I'm asking you to join me in a Let's Pretend game. These games are a great way for us to recreate a special mood or situation. With your help this morning we can tell the story of how the disciples learned to trust Jesus, especially when they felt frightened and forsaken. The story is commonly known as Jesus stilling the storm. To recreate the story I'll need a few of you to add some important sound effects. (*Choose a sufficient number of children to create the sound of wind, and others to create the sound of water; their cue is your mention of these elements. Have the two groups rehearse once or twice, mentioning that you will act as their volume control by raising or lowering your hand. Have the remaining children form themselves into a boat, leaving an empty space for Jesus. Be sure the sound-effects group is as close as possible to the "boat" so that they are part of the total drama.*)

At the end of the day, when the sun was setting, Jesus and his disciples began to cross the Sea of Galilee. Suddenly, out of nowhere, great black clouds covered the sky, and it grew very dark. The wind began to blow, and the sea began to rise and rock the boat. The disciples thought the storm would pass over soon, because they didn't see how it could become worse. But the storm grew even more fierce. The wind blew harder, and the waves poured over the side of the boat. The boat began to fill with water, and the disciples thought for sure their boat would sink and they would all be drowned.

They were frightened, and they felt alone! But Jesus was asleep in the back of the boat, his head resting on a cushion. Imagine that: while the wind blew fiercely and the waves slapped against the boat, Jesus was not even a little bit afraid because he had so much trust in God.

The disciples rushed to wake Jesus up. And when Jesus realized how frightened the disciples were, he commanded the wind and the water to be still — and they were quiet. Then Jesus turned to his disciples and asked them, "Why are you afraid? If you believe in God, know that God is all-powerful and can surely be trusted to care for us no matter what happens to us."

Reflection Note: The content of Let's Pretend stories is less important than the feelings they generate. Keeping in mind that children are particularly good at using their imaginations, you can think of a number of gospel stories that lend themselves to this mode of gospel-telling: the stories of the boy Jesus in the temple (Luke 2), the ten lepers (Luke 17), the feeding of the 5,000 (Matthew 14), the widow's mite (Luke 21), Jesus' visit to Mary and Martha (Luke 10), Jesus washing the feet of his disciples (John 13), and Jesus' cleansing of the temple (Matthew 21); and the parables of the great banquet (Luke 14), the sower (Mark 4), and of the lost coin, the lost lamb, and the lost son (Luke 15). Most of these stories also involve parabolic action through which the gospel is enacted. Be sure to define your characters carefully, as you do for role-playing stories; then children will feel more comfortable about participating. You should define the roles first, and then let children "feel" their parts. They can add their own definitions of their characters later on.

Visual Demonstrations

Given in the tradition of the parable, these sermons require the listeners' actual participation in the drama.

A Book Of Words/The Book Of Love

Text: John 20:30-31

Season: Any

Summary: The Bible is the book most important to us when we want to learn about love.

Props: A dictionary

The English language is made up of a lot of words. In school you're finding out just how many words there are. And when you get stuck, wondering how to spell a word or how to define a particular word, you find a dictionary. I happen to have one here — it's *Webster's Third International Dictionary*. It's quite a large book. In fact, it has 450,000 entries and 2,662 pages. As you can see, no one can know all the words in the English language, so it's very helpful to have a dictionary.

What do you think is the most *important* word in the English language? (*Have several children respond; a few will probably say "love."*) Those are all good answers, and some of you agree with me. I, too, think the word "love" is the most important word we have. Would anyone know how many times we find the word "love" in this dictionary? One time — that's right, one time — on page 1,340. So this dictionary isn't much help when it comes to finding the *most important* word, because it simply lists every word only once.

But if we turn to this book (*taking down the pulpit Bible*), which is just as big, we find that the word "love" is used almost 600 times! Let me read just a few of the important passages that speak about love:

You shall love *the Lord your God with all your heart,*
and with all your soul, and with all your might.
— Deuteronomy 6:5

You shall love *your neighbor as yourself.*
— Leviticus 19:18

God's steadfast love *endures forever.*
— Psalm 136:1

No one has greater love *than this to lay down one's*
life for one's friends. — John 15:13

Even if I speak in the tongue of men and of angels, but
have not love, *I am a noisy gong or a clanging cym-*
bal. — 1 Corinthians 13:1

There can be little doubt that "love" is the most important word in this book. And that's why it is often called the Book of Love.

I think we've learned something this morning that we already knew. The most important word in our lives is *love* — love that is given to us by God, our parents, our friends, and even by strangers. Life would be completely different if we could not give love and receive love. And we also learned that the Bible is *the* book to turn to when we want to learn more about love.

May the *love* of God the Creator, God the Redeemer, and God the Holy Spirit be with you all.

Adding A Drop Of Love

Text: Luke 21:1-4

Appropriate Day: The First Sunday of Lent or One Great Hour of Sharing

Summary: Take a few pennies, and add a drop of love — it can make a difference.

Props: An offering box, a clear bowl (e.g., a punch bowl) filled with water, an eye dropper, red food coloring, and two grain bags (available at hardware stores) — one full, labeled "U.S.A.," the other half empty

As part of my welcome this morning, I mentioned that this is the First Sunday of Lent. Lent is that period of forty days during which we prepare ourselves for Easter. And one of the ways this church prepares itself is with a special offering known as One Great Hour of Sharing. I have always liked that name because it has such a nice ring to it: as Christians we unite to help others in that special time, that "one great hour of sharing." You'll be getting a head start on the rest of us, because as you leave your Sunday school classes this morning, each of you will receive an offering box that looks like this one. (*Hold up box.*) Then, on Palm Sunday and Easter, all of us will bring our offering to church in order to celebrate One Great Hour of Sharing.

On my left and on my right are two grain bags. I brought these here today because they help us understand why we take this special offering during Lent. This bag is full, and it has on it the letters "U.S.A.," which stand for "the United States of America." And it's full because we who live in America and in _____, _____ (*name your city and state*), have a "full bag" of just about everything — food, clothing, housing, tools, grain, hospitals. The other bag is not even half full. It stands for the many people and many countries whose bag is almost empty of just about everything — food, clothing, housing, tools, grain, hospitals.

One Great Hour of Sharing is how we as Christians take some from our full bag and begin to fill this empty bag. And on _____ (*supply the date*) we will do just that: we will take your offering boxes and put them into this bag and see if we can fill it up.

During the next few weeks you will be dropping coins into your box, and many of those coins will be pennies. You might think that a few pennies or even a few dimes can't make much difference when there are so many needy people in the world, and when their needs are so great. It takes a lot of money to build a hospital or train a doctor. But I hope you will never believe that your offering, no matter how small, doesn't count.* Let's not forget that there are thousands — even millions — of Christians who will join us in this offering.

But even more important is the fact that as Christians we add something extra — God's love. With every penny or dollar, we mix in a little of God's love, just as the widow did when she gave her last penny. Not only does the Church bring food and medicine and trained men and women to help needy people, it also brings the Good News of God's love. And when people are hungry, lonely, scared, and hopeless, they really need to know that they are loved.

One drop of love, like one penny, doesn't seem like much. But let me show you that it can make a difference. How many drops of water would you say are in this punch bowl? (*Solicit several answers.*) A thousand million. That's a good guess, and since I didn't count the drops, I'm going to take your word for it. And to this bowl of a thousand million drops of water I'm going to add just a few drops of red food coloring — red because that's the color of love. When I add the drop and stir the water, those drops color the entire bowl of water.

Take a few pennies here and a few pennies there and add a few drops of love. It can make a difference. Believe me! Believe yourself! It can make a difference.

Reflection Note: The inspiration for this sermon came from a prayer by Helen Kromer in *For Heaven's Sake*, quoted by Jo Carr and Imogene Sorley in *Bless This Mess & Other Prayers*:

> *A drop in the bucket*
> *Is only a drop —*
> *A minor and moist detail;*
> *For a drop can't change*
> *The color and taste*
> *In a ten-quart watering pail.*
>
> *But if the drop*
> *Has the color of love*
> *And the taste of tears divine,*
> *One drop dropped into*
> *The vessel of life*
> *Can turn the water to wine. Amen.*

---

*The Fellowship of the Least Coin, an international fellowship of women based upon the story of the widow's mite, is a beautiful example of this belief.

Breakfast Of Champions

Text: Luke 2:52 (the *Good News Bible*): "Jesus grew both in body and in wisdom, gaining favor with God and men."

Season: Any

Summary: Part of growing up is to understand that dreams of being champions can prevent us from maturing as "complete" Christians.

Props: A box of Wheaties

I'm putting in front of you a box that's a familiar sight at many breakfast tables. But it's not just any old box of cereal — it's "the breakfast of champions." When I was growing up the ads led us to believe that every champion began the morning with a bowl of Wheaties. On the front or back of the box there was always a picture of a superstar who had set a new world's record in a sport like running, jumping, or swimming.

We all have dreams of becoming some kind of champion — a champion soccer player, a champion chess player, a champion piano player, or a champion mathematician. We all have a deep, burning desire to be the *best*, or if not the best there is, at least the best among our friends.

I once knew a boy who thought that if he ate enough Wheaties and trained very hard, he could become a great football player. But it wasn't to be. As he grew older, his body scarcely grew at all. And the other football players — well, they kept getting bigger and stronger. By the time this young man was a freshman in college, he was the smallest player on the team. It was a hard decision for him to make, but the next year he chose not to play football for the first time in many, many years. When he did that, he gave up his dream of being a great football player. But he also discovered that he had a lot more time to develop some of his other abilities and talents.

What am I trying to say to you? Am I telling you to give up your dreams of being a champion? No! Dreams are important and valuable because they make us set goals for ourselves — goals that make us work harder to become the very best we can be in a particular sport or activity. But our dreams of being champions can easily become so important that everything else becomes unimportant. As a consequence, we don't grow up in all the ways that Christians should.

We do not know much about Jesus as a young boy. But in the Gospel of Luke we do read that Jesus grew up in different ways. Luke tells us that Jesus grew big and strong, which says something about how his body changed. He also grew in wisdom and understanding, which means Jesus learned about the meaning of life from the Bible and other books, and from people. And, thirdly, Luke writes that Jesus grew in favor with God, which means that it was important whether or not he obeyed God. In other words, Jesus grew in many ways in order to become a complete person and a complete Christian.

That boy who didn't become a great football player is me. And as you can see, I did find something to do with my life besides play football. I still like my Wheaties with fruit. And I still like to play football and dream. But I no longer believe being a champion is the most important thing in my life. I'm content just keeping my body healthy and in good shape, and trying hard to continue to grow in wisdom and in favor with God.

I feel like offering a prayer to God. Will you join me? "Dear Lord, we give thanks that we are forever changing and growing. Bless us as we dream of being the best Christians we can become."

Humpty Dumpty Had A Great Fall

Text: 1 Corinthians 15:12-19 (Note the language of this passage. "Christ has been raised from the dead" as opposed to "he arose.")

Season: Easter

Summary: Death is real because it is final and irrevocable. Resurrection, therefore, demands a recreation.

Props: An egg, a hard surface (e.g., a cutting board)

Introduce the sermon by reviewing the events from Good Friday through Easter morning. Then see if they know the nursery rhyme.

> *Humpty Dumpty sat on a wall.*
> *Humpty Dumpty had a great fall.*
> *All the king's horses and all the king's men*
> *Couldn't put Humpty together again.*

Ask the children why the king, why no one, could put Humpty Dumpty back together again. If they do not know, tell them you will give them a hint. Show the egg. Talk a little about the egg and the mystery of life. Then demonstrate the nursery rhyme. Drop the egg onto a hard surface, such as a cutting board. For added dramatic effect, and other reasons, spread newspaper or plastic under the cutting board. You might even draw a face on the egg. Then drop the egg (no doubt to glee from some children and consternation from other children). Continue in this fashion:

Humpty Dumpty did indeed have a great fall. We could say that Humpty Dumpty died. Death is what happens when no one can put you back together again. When you die a process called decay begins and nothing, and no one, has the power to bring you back to life. And that is why we are sad when a pet dies or someone we love dies. It is final.

When Jesus died on the cross, there was nothing anyone could do to bring him back to life. His friends laid him in the tomb knowing the process of decay would begin. Their hearts were heavy with sadness. There was nothing they could do.

There was something God could do — and only God! God had the power to recreate Jesus. God has the power to put Humpty Dumpty back together again. The reason we are here today to celebrate Easter is to proclaim to the world: God did recreate Jesus Christ. God did not bring back Jesus from the dead like some mummy or a vampire. That really can't happen because death is final. When God recreated Jesus, Jesus was the same person but he was also different. Human words fail us. There aren't words to explain it. We will be thankful because we have this hope: the hope that even though you and I will die, God has the power to *recreate* us.

Reflection Note: It is likely that some will feel this sermon is too depressing for Easter. My reply is simply that the joy of Easter is measured against the stark reality of death. How can you have one without the other?

My One-tenth Box

Text: Genesis 28:18-22

Appropriate Day: Stewardship Sunday, any Sunday

Summary: Just as we budget money for our needs and wishes, we should set aside one-tenth of what we have for God.

Props: A box with a removable top (e.g., a popcorn container), some change

This morning I came prepared with my one-tenth box. What is a one-tenth box, you ask? I'll be happy to explain it to you.

When I was growing up, my parents kept a lot of boxes in a drawer. Every week when my father got paid, he would put a certain amount of money in each box. There was a box marked "clothing," a box marked "food," a box marked "housing," another box labeled "entertainment," and one last box marked "1/10th." (*Have a card marked with this fraction so that younger children can visualize one-tenth in their minds.*)

I thought I understood how my parents used the other boxes, but curiosity finally drove me to ask my parents about the one-tenth box. They explained to me that they used the boxes to budget their money each week so that they didn't spend so much on one need that they had nothing left for a different need. But the one-tenth box was different, because it wasn't meant to pay any of the family bills or provide us with money to see a movie or eat in a restaurant. Instead, it was God's share. The money in that box belonged to God, and each week we emptied the box and brought the money to church to be put into the offering.

In a minute I'm going to explain how you figure what a tenth of your allowance is. But first it's important that you know that the idea of a one-tenth box was not my parents' — it wasn't even the Church's idea. It's an idea that's even older than the Church itself, because it's mentioned in the Old Testament long before we read about the birth of Jesus and the beginning of the Christian Church. We know about the Ten Commandments that God gave to Moses. And we should also know about Jacob's promise to return to God one-tenth of what he had. It was something like a pledge on Jacob's part. If God would be with him and give him bread to eat and clothing to wear, Jacob would gladly return to God a tenth of what he had freely received from God.

And now we must learn how to figure what a tenth is. I came prepared this morning with some change. (*Ten pennies and twenty dimes work well for examples.*) If your parents gave you ten pennies, a tenth of that would be one penny; if they gave you ten dimes or a dollar, a tenth would be one dime; and if they gave you two dollars, a tenth would be two dimes. (*Illustrate your figuring with the pennies and dimes while you're talking.*) Who can tell me what a tenth of three dollars would be? (*Solicit some answers.*) Now you have the idea: you take the total and divide by ten, or figure a dime for every dollar of your allowance.

My parents taught me an important lesson with their labeled boxes. They knew, as I know now, that unless you have some place to set your money aside, it's going to get spent. And we must also remember to set aside the Lord's one-tenth even if we haven't been to worship.

As you can see, this sermon is not going to be finished when you leave for your Sunday school classes. You and your parents should discuss what an appropriate allowance would be for someone your age. And I hope that they'll help you make a one-tenth box, because Jacob's pledge is just like one of the Ten Commandments. We need to practice it all the time.

Reflection Note: This sermon illustrates another way to leave the conclusion open-ended, allowing the listener to complete the message. Jesus' encounter with the rich man who asked about eternal life ends in a similar fashion (Luke 18:18-23).

You Make Me Feel Like A Grapefruit

Text: Luke 19:1-10; Matthew 19:13-15

Season: Baptism, birthday of Martin Luther King, Jr.

Summary: The inclusion Jesus practiced did not require all of us to become the same but celebrates our differences.

Props: Several apples, a grapefruit, a banana, a few grapes

I have a short story for us today. One day an apple was coming down the road. Soon she was met by some other apples, and a few more. They all liked each other. They were friends. They formed a circle and talked with each other and played games and sang songs. (*Place apples appropriately.*)

Along came a grapefruit. (Hold it up.) He didn't really look like an apple. He was rounder and pinkish. But he saw the apples and asked if he could join their circle. They looked at one another and after a pause said, "All right." Even though the grapefruit was part of their circle, the apples continued to talk to each other and play games as if the grapefruit wasn't even there. The grapefruit thought to himself, "Why should I stay where I am not included," and left. (*Place apples and grapefruit appropriately.*)

Tell me, have you ever felt like a grapefruit? A little different? Left out? Maybe not even invited into a circle of friends? We all have. It's the feeling of being ignored, as if we weren't really there. The grapefruit wasn't included because he wasn't an apple. He wasn't red, but pink. There wasn't anything the grapefruit could do about that. That was how God made him.

Let me change the story by putting a figure of Jesus in the middle of the circle of apples. The grapefruit comes along and the apples invite him to join their circle. This time they talk with him and ask him to play and sing with them. And along comes a banana. She is tall and yellow and certainly doesn't look like an apple.

They open their circles and invite her in. Along come a few grapes. (*Place fruit appropriately.*)

When Jesus said, "Let the children come to me," he meant *all* the children — those with rounder faces, those who are taller, those who are smaller. Jesus did not try to change who we are and say we must first all become like apples. He stands in the center of the circles we form and invites everyone in.

(*A fitting conclusion would be to arrange the fruit as a fruit basket for the altar.*)

You Can't Steal A Spirit

Text: Matthew 2:1-12; 6:19-21

Appropriate Day: Epiphany or the Sunday after Christmas

Summary: The spirit of Christmas will last because every Sunday we celebrate God's gift of Jesus.

Props: A box of old toys (*wrap the box in holiday paper*)

Christmas is over, and that means the end of gift-giving. No more surprises. No more guessing what presents we're getting. Although it's true that Christmas Day won't come for another 3___ days, the Church celebrates the coming of the Wise Men from the East on January 6. This Sunday is known as Epiphany, and in the Greek Orthodox Church gifts are not unwrapped until this day in remembrance of the gifts that the Wise Men brought to the baby Jesus. I know we would like Christmas to last ... and last ... and last. But it can't — or can it?

On the chancel steps I see a Christmas present that's still wrapped, so maybe there is hope that Christmas can last. Let's open it and see what's in it. Let me see ... this box seems to be filled with several gifts, and they're not exactly new. My guess is that they're last year's Christmas presents. Actually, a few of them look like they're several years old. This game has lost its marbles, so it isn't much fun anymore. This book has seen better days, and it won't last much longer. And this doll has lost one of its arms.

You may say that wasn't much of a present — and you're right. I must confess that I was the one who brought the box in last night. I was thinking about one of my favorite Christmas television specials: *How The Grinch Stole Christmas*. Even though I've seen it many times, every Christmas I find myself watching it just one more time. As you probably remember, the Grinch tried to steal Christmas by taking all the presents and Christmas decorations

93

from the town of Who-ville, and when he left, it was clean as a whistle. But the Grinch couldn't actually steal Christmas, because Christmas is a spirit, and you can't steal a spirit. Even though the Grinch had taken everyone's presents, joyful sounds still filled the air on Christmas morning in Who-ville. Why? Because all the little Whos in the town were celebrating the birth of Jesus.

It was very easy and very natural to be excited about the presents you received from your parents. These old Christmas gifts are a reminder that in a few years even your new games and toys will find their way to the back of the closet or be thrown away. You may grow too old for them, or they may simply wear out.

But what about that other gift — the gift behind all the gifts we receive? This is the *love* of God, which gave us Jesus Christ, and the *love* of your parents, which gave you life. If anything is going to last, it will be the gift of love which is given day after day after day. That, of course, is the essence of the Christmas spirit. It is also the reason that the Grinch, mean as he was, could not steal the joy of Who-ville.

I truly hope that the spirit of Christmas will last for you. And I think it will, because every Sunday we celebrate God's great gift of Jesus. You may never have thought of Sunday in this way before. But every Sunday is like Christmas Day, when we open and give thanks for the gift of God's love, Jesus Christ.

May the *spirit* of Christmas be with you today, tomorrow, and every day to come.

94

Dramatic Participation

Given in the tradition of the parable, these sermons require the listeners' actual participation in the drama.

An Apple A Day

Text: Genesis 1:31

Season: Fall

Summary: To experience God's created world truly is to give thanks.

Props: One very red, delicious-looking apple, plus an apple for each child*

Somehow, the first apple of the season tastes the best. And the last apple, after we have had lots and lots of apples, doesn't taste nearly as good. Personally, I also enjoy much more the apples I pick myself. Not only is it fun to go to an orchard and see where the apples are growing; you have the advantage of picking the apples that look the best to you. And of all the apples I saw when I went to the orchard last Saturday, this one looked especially delicious. I'm going to put it aside for the moment. But while I was picking, I also had you in mind, so I've brought along an apple for each of you. (*Distribute apples.*) You may eat it, but I'm going to ask that you eat it in a very special way this morning.

First, I want you to hold the apple in your hands and polish it by rubbing it — give it a good shine. While you're doing this, feel it with your fingertips. Does it feel like anything else, or does it feel like only an apple can feel?

Now that you've polished your apple, hold it up to the light and look at its color. You'll discover that your apple is actually many different colors — not just red. How many different colors can you count? Are the colors unique to an apple?

We have felt the beauty of an apple through our fingertips, and seen it with our eyes. What about our ears? Let's listen to an apple. It's simple to do. Just take a small bite and strain your ears to catch every sound that's made as you sink your teeth into the skin of your apple. Is it a sound you have heard before? Describe the sound to yourself.

I'm wondering if any of you have taken the time to smell your apple. (*Children can do this while they are chewing the bite they've taken — which will take a while!*) Go ahead: give the apple a good sniff. This will be a test of how good your sense of smell is. Is it like any other smell? Can you describe it?

Finally, we use our last sense — that of taste. Close your eyes this time, take a small bite, and chew it slowly. Is your apple sweet or sour or a delicate balance of both? Keep your eyes closed and enjoy your bite as much as you can.

(*Turning to the congregation*) I'm sorry I didn't have an apple for each of you, but I'll bet this was the best apple you've ever "tasted."

When God finished creating the world, according to the book of Genesis, "God saw everything that God had made, and behold, it was very good." We don't realize *how* good until we take the time to discover the fullness of the beauty of each individual thing. I'm going to take this single apple I've been saving and place it on the communion table now. It will be part of my offering this morning. Let us give thanks, in prayer, as part of our offering:

"Dear God — wonderful Creator — we thank you for the beauty of just one apple: for its feel, its color, its smell, its sound, and its taste. Give us lots of apples, God, but let us still marvel at the beauty of just one apple. Amen."

---

*Raisins, peanuts, or other seasonal foods would work almost as well.

All The Glue In The World

Text: Genesis 1:31

Appropriate Day or Season: Earth Day, Spring

Summary: There is evidence of God's creating hand all around us. Let us wonder at and preserve what God has created.

Props: A flower and a very large bottle of glue. My favorite flower is Queen Anne's lace. Very common, it is often considered a weed but is actually a wild carrot. Take time to tell how it got its name; it looks like the lace worn by queens. A beautiful rose or a crocus is also effective.

Begin by asking for two volunteers, one younger and one older. Tell the younger child he has the easier task. Let him tear the flower into little pieces and put them into the cupped hands of the older child. Then turn to the older child and tell her that she has the more difficult task. Ask her to put the flower back together just as it was. After she gets over the shock, ask her if she could put the flower back if you gave her an hour, a whole day, or a month. Ask her if any person in the world could help her restore the flower to its original beauty. Finally, ask her if she could accomplish the task if she had all the glue in the world.

Take the pieces of the flower in your hands. As you are dropping the pieces onto the floor, say something like what follows below.

I wonder why it is that we are able to build spaceships that travel to the moon and back, but we cannot put a little flower back together again, not even with all the glue in the world. Could the reason be that *we* built the spaceship, but *God* gave us this flower? And God has not only given us this flower; God has created many,

98

many tokens of his love that we cannot put back after we have destroyed them.*

I would ask that you enjoy the springtime: take walks, listen and look at all of God's beauty that surrounds you. But please don't destroy anything you can't put back together.

Reflection Note: This sermon has other possible endings. For an older group the emphasis could be a demonstration that, at our very best, we as builders and inventors are only imitators of God's creativity. In either case, the sermon is a subtle demonstration of God's existence, but I would avoid making this aspect explicit. Why? Because explicit proofs only challenge the child/youth to argue about God rather than give thanks for the signs of God's creating power.

---

*Father Michael Quoist's popular book, *Prayers*, is dedicated to the theology that "if we knew how to look at life through God's eyes, we would see it as innumerable tokens of the love of the Creator seeking the love of his creatures."

Building A Church

Text: 1 Corinthians 3:5-11

Appropriate Day: Worldwide Communion Sunday, any Sunday

Summary: The Church is all kinds of people joined together, with Christ as its center.

Props: A hand-held mirror, a paper bag containing several different hats, and a cross

Everyone here knows what a church looks like. Would someone like to give me a description of a church? (*If the children who answer describe a building, remind them that they are giving descriptions of a building, not a congregation. You may offer to show them a picture of a church by holding up a hand mirror and letting them see their own reflection.*)

Some of you may even know a little song that does a good job of describing a church. It goes like this:

> *The church is not a building,*
> *The church is not a steeple,*
> *The church is not a resting place,*
> *The church is a people!*

I thought it would be fun if we could build a church this morning, and a very special church at that, because we want to build the Church as it includes people all over the world — the universal Church. Let's begin to build this "people church" by imagining who its members would be. As you think of different people who might belong to it, I'll ask you to come forward, describe the church member you're thinking of, and start forming a line. Just to give you a few ideas, I've brought in my bag of different hats. (*Give these to the younger children.*) The first one is a Native American headband — an important hat, because we need to remember Native Americans also belong to the Church. (*Come prepared with other hats, such as a king's crown, a farmer's hat, a coolie hat, a sombrero, etc. For other original ideas, use a Magic Marker to decorate plain hats made of cardboard. Solicit a variety of answers from the children before continuing.*)

Our church looks like it's complete, because it includes many different people, but something still isn't right. Everyone is standing in a line, but the Church is people who are doing exciting things. We need our church to be *in action.* (*Have children form action poses.*) And if the Church is going to be a true church, we must make one other change. We need a center, and that center is Jesus Christ. If we can all form a circle (*more or less*), I will put this cross in the center to symbolize the presence of Jesus Christ.

At last, our church is built. And I'd like all of you in the congregation to take a mental picture of what you see. A better-built church you will not see for a long time.

Reflection Note: In this sermon the listener-participant *carries* away with him a *picture* of the sermon. It is, therefore, "portable" and picturable — two ingredients for an effective sermon.

Fifty-two Card Pick-up

Text: John 13:1-11

Appropriate Time: Easter week*

Summary: Jesus gave us specific examples (demonstrations) of what it means to serve one another, one of which was washing the feet of his disciples.

Props: A deck of cards

As a minister I am always trying to relate what happened long ago to some experience with which you are familiar. I know a game that will help us understand what happened when Jesus and his disciples celebrated their last meal together.

I'll need a volunteer to play this game with me, which is a very simple card game. (*Show the cards as you choose a child to work with.*) Are you ready? This game is called "Fifty-two Card Pick-up." I start it by doing this (*fanning the cards all over the chancel*).

(*Wait until the child has picked up one or two cards.*) "Jim" (*address the child*), I really believe you would pick up all the cards, and some of your friends would probably help you. But I suspect that if I were your brother or sister or someone your age, you would tell me why I should pick the cards up, and why that was a rotten trick to play on you. But because I'm older than you, and your minister, and because this happened in worship on Sunday morning, you would probably pick up all the cards and give them back to me. What I want you to do, though, is sit here on the top chancel step while I pick up all the rest of the cards. (*As you are picking up the cards, pause every now and then and tell the story of John 13. Explain how Jesus poured water into a basin and one by one washed the feet of his disciples, and explain how Peter protested.*)

Jesus washed his disciples' feet because he wanted to give them a visible demonstration of what it means to serve others even if you don't have to. (*I have in mind Martin Luther's statement: "A Christian is the most free lord of all, subject to none; a Christian is the most dutiful servant of all, subject to everyone."*) And so I give to you this visible demonstration of my love for each of you, and my willingness to be your servant.

Reflection Note: As in Jesus' use of parabolic actions such as the washing, the proclamation is the action, not the words. Any further explanation cuts off the process necessary for the individual to remember the image you have created, and prevents it from freely playing itself out in his or her life. Of course, you could wash the feet of several of the children.

---

*A different text for this sermon could be Jesus' command about forgetting ourselves and carrying our cross (Mark 8:34-38). This would be an appropriate message for Halloween or April Fools' Day, because the accent would be upon a trick that becomes an example.

Yesterday I Stomped On A Frog

Text: Isaiah 42:5; Exodus 20:13; Genesis 1:24

Season: Any

Summary: We should make a conscious commitment not to kill another living thing.

Props: A bell that a child can ring (e.g., a dinner bell or hand bell)

Some of you may have heard of Albert Schweitzer. He was awarded the Nobel Peace Prize in 1952 and was a very talented person: he was a marvelous organist, a gifted preacher, and a New Testament scholar. Yet, in spite of his accomplishments, Albert Schweitzer was still not convinced that he was doing enough with his life, so he decided to return to medical school and become a doctor. His dream was to become a medical missionary — and he did. He was well-known for his work in Africa, where he built a famous hospital in a place called Lambarene.

When he was about eight years old, Albert Schweitzer had a very unusual experience. He was out playing one day when some friends asked him to join them; they were going to shoot birds with their slingshots. At first Albert didn't want to go, but after repeated pleading he gave in. Creeping up behind a rock, Albert took aim to shoot a songbird, but just then he heard a church bell ringing. It was, in Albert's own words, like a voice from heaven. He threw down his slingshot, horrified at the thought of having come so close to killing a harmless creature. And in that moment there was born in Schweitzer's heart what would become one of the great ideas of modern man: reverence or respect for life.

I have here a bell, and in a minute I'm going to invite you to come forward and ring it. And as you ring it, you must pledge to try not to hurt another living thing.

But you may be saying to yourself, "I don't know if I can keep that pledge." Let me tell you another short story about a six-year-old boy who refused to ring the bell.* After considerable urging, and with downcast eyes, he explained, "I don't believe I deserve to ring the bell, because yesterday I stomped on a frog." The important thing to remember is that you're going *to try* not to hurt another living thing. Maybe you won't always be able to keep your promise, but if you're willing to try, I invite you to come forward and ring this bell.

Reflection Note: Later I wondered why I didn't use the bell in the church belfry. That would certainly be more dramatic, and would give the children the chance to decide, out of public view, if they really want to ring the bell. (*They could do this after Sunday school.*)

Bear in mind the learning pyramid (Part I, p. 29) — the act of ringing would reinforce the verbal story. The church bell might then become a symbol to the children, because every time they heard the bell ring (or rang it themselves), they would remember the story of Albert Schweitzer and would mentally participate in the story's reenactment.

---

*In the Albert Schweitzer Friendship House, founded by Mrs. Erica Anderson just outside Great Barrington, Massachusetts, there is a tower in which hangs a bell with a long rope. Here children are invited to make their pledge after they have seen a moving film (made by Mrs. Anderson) about the last years of Dr. Schweitzer's life.

What To Do With A Chocolate Chip Cookie?

Text: Isaiah 58:6-10; Matthew 25:35

Season: Halloween Crop Walk or any

Summary: Whether or not we will share what we have with others is a decision each of us must consciously make.

Props: Several oversized chocolate chip cookies; several construction-paper-and-string signs, printed with the names of both well-to-do and poor countries, that children can hang around their necks.

With a few words of introduction, read the passage from Isaiah. Then divide the children into groups of about five to ten (*ideally three to four groups*). Give each group a sign, a few printed with the names of prosperous countries, the others printed with the names of poor countries. Next explain to the children, "Today we're going to play a game — a very serious game, though. Some of you will represent countries with plenty of food, and others will represent countries with very little food."

Now give a cookie to each group representing one of the prosperous countries, and tell the children representing the poor countries that they get nothing. (*Don't give cookies to very young children. Give them only to children who can act as leaders of their groups.*) Say nothing more (*don't overexplain or lead*); just wait. Depending upon what happens — and especially if nothing happens — you might say to the representatives, "You have a few minutes to decide what to do with your cookies."

The conclusion must be ad-libbed. Most likely the representatives of the prosperous countries will give away some of the cookies to friends who then might share with others.

When the distribution is complete, summarize the experience by recalling the scripture passage. You might conclude with these words: "Jesus said to his friends, 'When I have gone away and you try to find me, you will see me in the eyes of every man, woman, and child who is hungry.' "*

---

*Paraphrase of Matthew 25:44-45. Mahatma Gandhi once said, "To millions who have to go without two meals a day, the only acceptable form in which God dare appear is food."

Pantomime And Echo

These sermons require the listeners to process nonverbal clues and use their imaginations. The outer voice is turned off so the inner voice can be turned on.

Love Conquers All

Text: Romans 12:17-21 or Luke 23:32-34

Appropriate Day or Season: Easter, any Sunday

Summary: Forgiveness is that kind of Christian love that can overcome hate.

Props: Five or more helium-filled balloons (one, which may be larger than the others, has a cross on it); a large pin (i.e., a hatpin); five or more actors (in the traditional white face of the mime, if you like); a piano player

Begin by reading the Scripture passage.

The pantomime is this: The first actor comes dancing down the aisle holding the largest balloon. Her joy is obvious as she moves about the chancel. She pauses to trace the cross on her balloon. To the sound of light, joyful music, others come dancing down the aisles, but without balloons. When the first actor sees that they are without balloons, she goes to one side of the chancel where a handful of balloons hang. She then gives each mime a balloon. Their smiles grow bigger when they receive this gift.

Note: It is important here, that the mimes express joy in the giving and receiving of the balloons and not in their possession. To symbolize this, they might also exchange balloons. The balloon with the cross ends up with the first actor.

The music now changes from joyful praise to melodrama; although no one knows it, the villain is hiding behind the pulpit. He subtly appears and gradually approaches the first mime. As the other actors become aware of his approach, they back away. Then, with his hatpin poised high, the villain strikes and breaks the balloon with the cross. With the exception of the villain, everyone is sad. They bow their heads and pull down their balloons. The music becomes dirge-like.

At first hesitant and doubtful, the actor closest to the first mime hands her a balloon. (*She may choose to draw a cross on her balloon as she did before, but it is not necessary.*) Gradually joy returns as the mimes trade balloons; the music changes, too.

The villain looks disconcerted, even angry. All the actors again back away, leaving only the villain and the first mime center-stage on the chancel. She notices the dejection of the villain, and, after thoughtful consideration, she gives her balloon to him. At first he refuses it, but then changes his mind. Now all the actors begin to return to the chancel, and several offer their balloon to the first mime. The music now becomes victorious.

The pantomime can end in a variety of ways. The mimes might give balloons to the congregation. Our choice was to ask the congregation to join in the singing of "Pass It On" by Kurt Kaiser.

Reflection Note: Because a pantomime is wordless, the pictures painted by the actors become amplified, and are crucial. Thus the mimes should freeze their significant poses for two to four seconds so they can "set." The observers become active participants because they must supply the narrative to match the action — hence the power of pantomime. The symbolism in this sermon isn't necessary; it's added so that the pantomime can operate at several levels simultaneously (see "Targeting Your Sermon" in Part I).

Overcoming Temptation

Text: Exodus 20 (commandments about stealing and coveting)

Season: Any

Summary: The way to overcome temptation is by praying and turning our backs on the thing we desire.

Props: A table and chair; you in the traditional white face of the mime, if you choose to apply it.

Today I'm going to tell a story through pantomime, which is a story without words. And because the words are missing, we gain a better sense of the inner feelings of the actor. This particular pantomime is about three words: "steal," "covet," and "temptation." According to the eighth commandment, we should not steal what belongs to another person, and according to the tenth commandment, we should not covet or desire with our heart what belongs to another. And temptation is that feeling, that impulse, that ever-present itch to disobey God.

Scene I
You shall not steal. (*Announce this.*)
Begin by playing a game with yourself at the table (e.g., ball and jacks, cards).
Suddenly, your eyes fall upon something you want,* and you begin to grin.
You walk around this object, and your grin becomes wider.
You look to see if you are being watched.
You quickly grab the object and run back to your table and chair.
You put the object on the table, staring at it and grinning.
Gradually, your stare changes, and your grin is not so wide.
No matter what you do or where you move, that object reminds you of your disobedience. Your grin disappears.

Scene II

You shall not covet. (*Announce this.*)

You are playing the same game.

As your eyes wander, they're attracted to something.

Your whole body is attracted to this object (or person), and you begin to grin.

You circle it, and your hands reach out and almost grab it. Your smile gets bigger.

You return to your table and chair, but all the time you look over your shoulder and grin.

No matter what you do or where you move, your eyes still return to the thing you desire.

Sitting in your chair, you are transfixed by this object. Your grin slowly turns to despair.

(*You may wish to stop the pantomime here and ask the children what they felt and learned and how they would explain the difference between stealing and coveting: e.g., coveting is stealing with one's heart. If we were to be satisfied with being good teachers, we might say, "Well done," and conclude this sermon. But since we are also preachers of the Good News, we present a third scene which illumines the grace God gives us to overcome temptation.*)

Scene III

Overcoming temptation. (*Announce this.*)

You are playing the same game.

As your eyes wander, they are attracted to something.

You get up and begin circling this object, grinning.

Your hands shake, and your body trembles with desire.

Using your will, you turn your back on the object and begin walking away.

As you walk, your head and body begin to turn back to the object, but you control them.

You feel the pull of the object so strongly that you have to hold your head with your hands to keep it from turning toward the object.

You stop and offer a prayer.

You reach your table and sit down.

113

You realize that the desire to look is no longer so strong.
You are able to return to your game and smile without being concerned with the object. You have forgotten it.

---

*A real objective if younger children are your target audience; otherwise stick
with the use of one's imagination. The object could be placed on the table and
the game played on the floor, but everything should be visible for all to see.

The Good Samaritan,* Part I

Text: Luke 10:25-37

Season: Any

Summary: God's love makes it possible for anyone to be a Good Samaritan.

Introduction: One day Jesus was tested with this question: "If I am supposed to love my neighbor as myself, who is my neighbor?" Jesus answered by telling a story — this story. I ask that you pay attention because I'll be telling the story again and asking you to join me by being an echo.

I am who I am (*point to yourself*).
One day I put on my sandals (*pretend to put on sandals*),
and my traveling cloak (*mimic slipping arms into loose cloak*).
I took my money bag (*hold imaginary bag in fist*),
and hid it in my belt (*mimic tucking it in wide belt*).
Then I started on my way (*walk in place*)
from Jerusalem to Jericho (*sweep arm in wide arc*),
up hill and down hill (*lean backward, lean forward*),
past dark caves where robbers might hide (*look fearful*).
I pretended I wasn't afraid (*stand straight, hands clasped behind back*);
but all of a sudden I was surrounded by robbers (*arms go up*),
and one of them hit me (*crouch as if to protect self*);
that was the last thing I remember (*bend further down*).
After a while (*cup hand to ear*),
I heard footsteps (*cross arms, slapping hands on arms*).
The footsteps grew louder (*slap more loudly*).
It was a priest (*stop slapping; hold arms akimbo*).
He said, "Can't stop now, sonny" (*look down and shake head*),
"but I'll come back later" (*wave good-bye*).

115

After a while (*cup hand to ear*),
I heard new footsteps (*raise hands to shoulder level; snap fingers*).
It was a Levite (*continue snapping fingers*).
He said, "Too bad, too bad" (*shake head*);
then he went on his way (*wave good-bye*).
Soon I heard other footsteps (*slap thighs, one after the other*).
It was a Samaritan on a donkey (*continue thigh-slapping*).
"Whoa! Need any help?" (*mimic pulling reins, lean over and look down*).
Then he jumped down (*jump up and down once*),
and took off his cloak (*mimic taking off cloak*),
tore it into strips (*pretend to tear strips of cloth*),
and bandaged my wounds (*mimic rolling bandages on wounded areas*).
He lifted me onto his donkey (*mimic lifting and placing body gently*),
and slowly we went on our way (*slap thighs more slowly*),
until we came to an inn (*mimic pulling back on reins*).
He carried me inside (*arms outstretched in carrying position*),
and laid me on a bed (*pretend to place body on bed*).
"Here is some money," he said to the innkeeper (*mimic taking coins from bag*);
"I will pay all that is owed" (*pretend to tuck money bag back in belt*).
Then he went on his way (*slap thighs*).

Now I ask you (*point finger at listeners*),
which one loved me as a neighbor? (*Point as if to three distinct persons*)
The priest who said, "Can't stop now, sonny" (*hold arms akimbo*);
the Levite who said, "Too bad, too bad" (*snap fingers once*);
or the Good Samaritan (*slap hands on thighs*)?
Go thou (*point to one side of congregation*),
and do likewise (*swing arm to other side of congregation*).

---

*Adapted from "Living the Word," Level 4 (Winter 1979-1980), JED curriculum.

The Good Samaritan, Part II
The Loving Warlock*

Introduction: This time we'll retell the story of the Good Samaritan as Jesus might have told it to us. You now have a feeling for the way the story will be told. So be my echo and repeat the same words and actions after me.

I am who I am (*point to yourself*).
One day I put on my shoes (*pretend to put on shoes*),
and my overcoat (*mimic slipping arms into coat*).
I took my money (*open hand*)
and hid it in my jeans pocket (*slip hand into back pocket*).
Then I got on my ten-speed racer (*imitate climbing on bike*),
and started on my way (*walk in place*)
from _____ to _____ (*name two local communities;
    walk in place*),
up hill and down hill (*lean forward; lean backward*),
past big trees where muggers might hide (*look fearful*).
I pretended I wasn't afraid (*stand straight, hands clasped behind
    back*).
But all of a sudden (*arms go up*),
muggers jumped out at me (*crouch as if to protect self*)!
One of them hit me (*kneel, head down*);
that was the last thing I remember (*bend further down*).
After a while (*cup hand to ear*)
I heard footsteps (*cross arms, slapping hands on arms*).
The footsteps became louder (*slap more loudly*),
It was one of the local ministers (*stop slapping; hold arms akimbo*).
He said, "Can't stop now, sonny" (*look down and shake head*),
"but I'll come back later" (*wave good-bye*).
After a while (*cup hand to ear*),
I heard new footsteps (*raise hands to shoulder level, snap fingers*).
It was a local schoolteacher (*continue snapping fingers*).

She said, "Too bad, too bad" (*shake head*);
then she went on her way (*wave good-bye*).
Soon I heard the sound of a motorcycle (*make sound of engine*).
It was a tough-looking Warlock (*hold thumbs up*).
He said, "Hey, need any help?" (*lean over and look down*)
Then he jumped down (*jump up and down once*),
and tore off his leather jacket (*pretend to take off coat*),
and wrapped it around me (*move hands in circular wrapping motion*).
Then he lifted me onto his motorcycle (*mimic lifting and placing body gently*),
and we went slowly on our way (*hold hands as if gripping handlebars, make sound of engine*).
Soon we came to a Holiday Inn (*make sound of screeching brakes*).
He carried me inside (*arms outstretched in carrying position*),
laid me on a bed (*pretend to place body on bed*),
and paid the manager $100 (*mimic handing out a few bills*).
"Take care of my buddy," he said (*one hand outstretched, palm up*).
"I'll take care of the cost" (*pat back pocket where money would be*).
Then this kind Warlock went on his way (*hold hands as if gripping handlebars*).

Now I ask you (*point finger at congregation*),
which one loved me as a Christian (*point to three imaginary people*):
the minister who said, "Can't stop now" (*hold arms akimbo*);
the schoolteacher who said, "Too bad, too bad" (*snap fingers once*);
or the Warlock (*hold hands as if gripping handlebars, make sound of engine*)?
You must go (*point to one side of congregation*),
and do likewise (*sweeping motion to the other side*).

Reflection Note: The parable of the Good Samaritan is ripe with exegetical problems, but it is sufficient to note that it has two themes. There is first the theme of what it means to be a good neighbor. If this had been the story's only purpose, it would have been far better if the wounded man had been the Samaritan, because it would have more perfectly illustrated that Christian love has no limits (i.e., it includes one's enemies). But when the half-breed Samaritan becomes the compassionate one, rather than the two authority figures known for doing good, then the parable is about reversal and judgment; it is a story not so much about doing a good deed (cf. 2 Chronicles 28:1-15) as about the inbreaking of the Kingdom that reverses our expectations about *who* can be good.

For this reason I've chosen to tell the story twice. The first version emphasizes the theme of being a good neighbor ("Go thou and do likewise"), and the second highlights the embarrassing realization of *who* was the good neighbor to the man who fell among the robbers. (Which of these three, do you think, proved neighbor to the man who fell among the robbers?) The story's point is that we must decide, based upon our particular situation, who might be the least likely to hear the gospel and respond with Christian compassion.

Read as a story, "The Good Samaritan" is a model of what it means to be a good neighbor; told as a parable, it invites us to abandon our usual way of behaving by *reversing* our perception of the way things always seem to be.

---

*The Warlocks are a motorcycle gang in the city where I used to live. You will have to substitute a name that children in your church would recognize.

Storytelling

These stories have a well-defined plot and characters. Good storytelling is an art form and is the most difficult of the forms to use successfully, but there is nothing like a good story told well.

A Prince In Disguise*

Text: Matthew 25:31-46 (44-45)

Appropriate Day: All Saints' Day, any Sunday

Summary: Treat everyone as if he or she were Jesus.

Preparation: Spend a few minutes discussing what a disguise is, and then read or summarize the Bible passage. The story will then have a context, and you won't need to interpret it or offer explanation.

Today I want you to listen very carefully to a story. After I've finished it you'll have to think about it and perhaps ask your parents about its meaning. It's called "A Prince In Disguise."

Once, long ago (but not too long ago) in a faraway place (but not too far away), there lived a very special king. He was, by any standard, very kind, very just, and very wise. Even though his kingdom had no boundaries, for it was large beyond imagination, everyone in it knew the king was a loving father. Once a week he would step into his royal carriage, and his royal coachman and royal horses would carry him through the streets. And of course all the young men would bow and all the young ladies would curtsy as the king passed by.

Although this king was very, very rich, there was one thing he did not have, and because he did not have it, he wanted it more than anything else in the world. Can you guess what it was? That's right — he wanted a son (daughter). The king prayed every morning and every evening that a son would be born to him and his wife, the queen, for what good would his kingdom be if he did not have an heir who would become the next king (queen)? Oh, how he prayed and wished for a son.

And one day it happened: the queen gave birth to a child, and it was a boy! The good news spread quickly throughout the kingdom, and the people were happy and thankful; now there would be a prince who would someday be the next king.

The years passed, and the little baby boy grew to be a little prince. And once a week the prince and his father the king would step into the royal carriage, and the royal coachmen and the royal horses would carry them through the streets.

Because the king had only one son and because he loved him with all his heart, he was especially careful to make sure that no harm would befall his son. In fact, he built a very tall stone wall around the castle so that the prince would see nothing of the ugly, evil things that happened in the world beyond it. But the prince was curious, just like boys and girls about your age, and one day he decided that he wanted to see what the world was like beyond the stone wall. After carefully disguising himself, he slipped away from the castle. He walked down dusty roads and through village streets. He saw the clear blue skies, enjoyed the beautiful flowers, and felt the gentle rain just as he did behind the stone wall; but he also saw people stealing and cheating one another, and mothers too poor to feed their babies.

Of course, the king was frantic when he discovered that his dearly beloved son was lost in the great world beyond the castle walls. So the king gathered together all his messengers and told them to go to every street corner and alleyway and read to the people this solemn declaration: My son, the prince, is lost somewhere among you. Will you help me find him?

Young and old, male and female, the people looked high and low to find the prince, because they knew the king would be forever grateful if they found his son. But no one could find the prince, because he had disguised himself to look just like everyone else. And because the prince could be anyone, the people decided it was best to treat everyone as if he were the prince.

Even to this day the prince still walks the streets, and you may by chance meet him someday.

Reflection Note: I prefer to leave the story open-ended for the reasons discussed in "Overhearing The Gospel" in Part I. The success of this story doesn't depend on its analogy to the story of

Jesus in Matthew 25. It can stand by itself in the minds of younger children as a story of a prince who learns the truth about this world and of a father's love for his son. Older children and those adults who "happen" to be listening in will catch the analogy. True, our primary responsibility is to target children's sermons for children, but we should never forget the powerful dynamics that develop when others listen in. This is one very good reason why the Sunday scripture lesson(s) should serve as the basis for both children and adult sermons.

---

*Or princess, if you prefer. Change the "son," "boy," and masculine pronoun references to "daughter," "girl," and female pronoun references.

Baa-Baa

Text: Luke 15:1-7 ("... until he finds it")

Season: Any

Summary: God is a good shepherd who searches until she finds the one who is lost.

Props: A shepherd's crook; a flannel board and figures: a shepherd (male or female figure), a lamb and a flock of sheep, a sun, and a black piece of felt (or similar material) to represent the darkness. This is a story that can be told with flannel graph figures, or in the spirit of Jerome Berryman's style with felt underlay and cutout figures, or without props but with lots of dramatic action.

If you have ever seen a real lamb, which is soft and cuddly, you can't help but want to give it a big hug. Have you ever thought what it would be like to be a little lamb? If you were a lamb, you would need someone to watch over you, someone to keep you from getting lost — a shepherd. And a shepherd might carry a crook like this one, which a friend (*supply the name*) lent me. The crook is used by shepherds both to ward off any would-be attackers, like a wolf, and to pull back a lamb if it begins to wander away. (*Illustrate its use.*) Like most children I know, lambs have a way of wandering off and becoming lost. If the shepherd sees this happening, she will use her crook and gently pull or nudge the lamb back toward the flock.

My story this morning is about a lamb named Baa-Baa who gets lost, and about a good shepherd. (*Arrange the figures on the flannel board.*) I'm telling this story because Jesus told a similar story when he told us who God is.

Our story begins on a day in spring. The sun was brightly shining, the clouds were puffy and white, and Baa-Baa was as happy as she could be. It was a beautiful day, and the grass was green and especially sweet. She never imagined that something could go wrong.

Baa-Baa thought to herself how nice it was to have a good shepherd to watch over the flock. Today she was leading them to a new field. Baa-Baa had never been here before, but then she had never been much of any place before. She noticed that the sun was not as high in the sky as it had been, which meant that it would soon be getting dark, but it didn't seem to matter. Baa-Baa just kept on munching the sweet grass, not even noticing that she was moving farther and farther away from the rest of the flock. And in no time at all Baa-Baa was eating grass all by herself.

It was quite a long time before Baa-Baa realized what had happened. The flock had gone off without her, or she had gone off without the flock. Whatever had happened, it was time to start looking for the other sheep. She tried very hard to find them, because she didn't want to be scolded for getting lost, but the harder she tried, the more lost she became. Now it was getting dark, and Baa-Baa began thinking about all the terrible things that could happen to her. What if night came, and she was still lost? She might fall and break a leg, she would have nothing to drink, she would get cold, and the wolves — she didn't want to think about the wolves. It no longer mattered if the shepherd would scold her for getting lost; Baa-Baa just wanted to be found.

Then she thought, I wonder if the good shepherd is looking for me? Would she try to find me in the night? Would she leave the other sheep, safely in their pen, and come after me? *Would she do that to find just one lamb?*

Suddenly, the darkness came in all its blackness (*illustrate*), and Baa-Baa couldn't see anything. There was nothing she could do but wait, wait and find out if the good shepherd cared enough to come looking for just one forgetful lamb that had gotten lost.

Baa-Baa had no idea what time it was when she heard a noise. Her first thought was that the wolves had found her. But then she heard someone calling her name: "Baa-Baa. Baa-Baa." She started running, trying to find the voice that called to her. Before she could see the shepherd, she heard footsteps — fast footsteps. And when at last the figure in the dark became clear, the shepherd was not

126

only calling her name, but was running toward her. When she reached Baa-Baa, she lifted her onto her shoulders.

They were on their way home — Baa-Baa was sure of that. She also knew how good it felt to be safe again in the arms of one who loved her very much. Then Baa-Baa noticed that the good shepherd wasn't carrying her crook. This time she didn't need her crook; she had come herself to find one lost and lonely lamb.

And that is the end of the story, although it isn't really *my* story. It is Jesus' story, the one he told when he wanted to explain to others what God is like. God is like the good shepherd who will not rest until she finds you.

Reflection Note: I didn't try to build into this story an analogy between being lost and being "lost" in sin. Certainly this is part of the biblical account, but the sermon is focused on the single experience of knowing a God who cares enough to leave the 99 in order to find the one that is lost. In order not to make this an analogical story, the word "like" is omitted (Jesus is like a shepherd). To make this story even more experiential, begin with a discussion of how it feels to be lost.

----

*I have made the shepherd in this story female because the feminine side of God is overshadowed by male images. I would also note that in the following parable, that of the lost coin, it is the woman who seeks diligently "until she finds it."

Devils Are For Sale, Aren't They?

Text: Matthew 6:13 ("And lead us not into temptation ..."); Mark 14:38

Season: Any

Summary: It is better to be busy for the Lord than idle for the Devil.

Props: Your best storytelling hat

Today I have a most intriguing story for you. I must admit that it's not my own story but one told many, many times by very wise men called Zen Masters.*

About 200 years ago a gentleman who lived in a large house by the side of the road decided to go to the marketplace. As he was walking down a back street, he noticed a very unusual sight: a merchant stood beside a cage with a sign overhead which read "Devil for sale." As he grew closer, the gentlemen could see it was a yellow-skinned devil about the size of a large dog, with a tail and two long, sharp fangs. He sat quietly in his cage, gnawing on a bone.

After the gentleman regained his composure, he asked the merchant whether his devil was for sale. "Oh," said the merchant, "the devil isn't mine, but of course he is for sale. I want you to know this is an excellent devil — strong, hard-working, and able to do almost anything you ask of him. He knows how to cut firewood, clean house, wash dishes — he can even mend clothing. And my price isn't too high. If you give me $200, he's yours."

The gentleman thought it was a fair price, so he paid the merchant and started on his way, carrying the devil in its cage.

"One moment," the merchant shouted. "Because you haven't bargained with me, I want to tell you something about this devil

128

you ought to know. He is a devil, of course, and devils are no good. You know that, don't you?"

"Everyone knows that," the gentleman replied sharply. "Besides, you said he was an excellent devil."

"I did at that, and he will do everything I said he could do," replied the merchant. "I only wanted to warn you that you must keep him busy from sunup to sundown. If he has time to spare, time when he has nothing to do, then he's dangerous."

"If that's all," the gentleman said, "I will take my devil home and put him to work."

At first, everything went smoothly. Every morning the gentleman would call the devil, who bowed down obediently in front of him. The devil would then do everything the gentleman ordered him to do. If he wasn't working, he was playing or resting, but whatever he did, he was always obeying his master's orders.

Then, after some months, the gentleman met an old friend in the city, and because of the thrill of seeing an old acquaintance he forgot everything. He and his friend went to a cafe and started drinking to their friendship. Next they went to a nightclub where they had more drinks and spent the rest of the evening, having a grand time. The next morning the gentleman woke up in a strange place. At first he didn't know what had happened, but gradually it all came back to him. He then remembered his devil, and rushed home. When he reached his street, he smelled something burning, and saw smoke coming from his house. He stormed into his kitchen, where he found the devil sitting on the wooden floor. He had made an open fire and was roasting the neighbor's dog on a spit.

Of course, devils aren't really for sale, as we know. This story is just a dramatic way of teaching us something we ought to know about evil. We know all too well that we get into more trouble when we have nothing to do. It seems the dark side of us is always waiting for its opportunity to show itself, and that opportunity so often comes when our hands are idle and we have nothing constructive to do. This is when we are tempted to pick a fight, to destroy something that someone else has made, or simply to be mischievous.

That phrase from the Lord's Prayer — "and lead us not into temptation" — is one we repeat so often that we never give it a second thought. Perhaps we should make this request more consciously. And might we not also ask God to keep us busy all day doing what is positive and constructive? If we are busy for the Lord and his good, then we will in truth be delivered from all evil.

Reflection Note: A good story does not need to be explained. Since this is a good story, I hesitate to add any kind of explanation. But because of the stark images, I would target this sermon for older children/youth and include a warning that it is about the dark side of each of us.

---

*This story is adapted from Janwillem van de Wetering's *The Empty Mirror* (Boston: Houghton Mifflin, 1947, pp. 107-109). Even in its adapted form, this story is for older children and young people who are able to understand it as a pictorial representation of inner urges.

Looking For The Devil

Text: Ephesians 6:13; Proverbs 8:13

Season: Any

Summary: The evil we seek to cast out is the evil we find in ourselves.

Props: A good picture of the Devil*

Today I've brought along a picture of someone everyone will recognize, and yet I'll bet that no one has ever seen this person. (*Show the picture and wait for responses.*) It seems that I was right on both counts. Everyone knew this was a picture of the Devil even though no one has actually ever seen him. It makes me wonder if we would really know the Devil if we met him or her or it.

One day, when I was a little boy, I crawled out of bed and went looking for the Devil. And where do you think I found him? I didn't find him in a hole. And I didn't find him in a dark corner. I didn't find a mean-looking monster, red all over with a pitchfork and tail. In fact, I didn't find anything I could grab and shake and tell to get out of my life. I wonder why I didn't find the Devil when I went looking for him?

You know what I think? When I was a young child I didn't look in the right place — I forgot to look inside myself. Now that I'm older I believe the Devil is actually all the evil in the world that is in all of us. The Devil can be the little voice in us that tempts us to say mean things and to do things that hurt other people.

Have you ever said to yourself, "I know I shouldn't be doing this, but I'm going to do it anyway"? And when you get caught or you think about the awful thing you did, you say to yourself, "Gee, I wish I hadn't done that." That, my friends, is how evil works, and how it stays alive.

131

The day I went looking for the Devil and found him inside my heart, I also discovered that I could chase him out, because I found that God's spirit also lives in my heart. And I discovered something even more amazing: that when there is love in my heart, there is no room left for evil to trouble me. So whenever I'm tempted to be mean or unkind, I just think about how God loves me, and in no time at all my evil thoughts are gone.

It's not very often that I write a poem, but here's one that fits the occasion:

The Day I Went Looking for the Devil

I didn't find the Devil in a deep, dark hole,
And I didn't find him spying from a big high pole;
Instead I found him talking in whispers to me,
Saying how much fun being mean would be.
But thanks to God, I found a great art,
A way to get the Devil out of my heart:
I think a kind thought, I do a good deed,
And evil goes down to death and defeat.

Reflection Note: It's important that we don't end sermons on a negative (imperative) note; we need to offer a positive (indicative) possibility. Compare this sermon with Scene III of the pantomime "Overcoming Temptation."

Let's resolve to double our efforts to underscore the power of the gospel to lift us our of our usual condition. Because we are so good at describing the human predicament, we often neglect to demonstrate the new things possible in Christ.

---

*Valerie Stalder's *Even the Devil Is Afraid of a Shrew* contains some marvelous pictures of a devil.

The Story Of Tom Gobble

Text: 1 Chronicles 16:34; Psalm 145:10-13

Appropriate Day: Thanksgiving

Props: A flannel board and pictures of a small turkey and a big turkey

Preparation: Begin by briefly describing what the word "greedy" means (i.e., "to grab").

Tom was the smallest turkey in Farmer Jones' barnyard (*put his picture up*), but Tom was a very greedy little turkey. At night he was always the first one in the barn so that he could get the best bed. In the morning he was always the first one out the door so that he could be the first to clean himself in the bath. And at mealtime he was always the first to gobble up the food. Tom Gobble was a sight to see when it was time to eat: he would spread his feathers and run through the barnyard, screaming, "Gobble, gobble, gobble, you'd better get out of my way!" As days turned into months and Tom continued his greedy ways, he grew bigger and bigger and bigger, until one day he was the biggest turkey in the barnyard (*change pictures*).

Because Thanksgiving Day was coming, Farmer Jones was sizing up his turkeys to see which one would make the best Thanksgiving dinner. Well, you can guess what happened. When Tom Gobble saw Farmer Jones coming after him, he wished he hadn't been so greedy — but his wishing had come too late. Farmer Jones fixed him for Thanksgiving dinner, and that afternoon all the barnyard animals began to sing this little song:

> *O, Tom Gobble, you had to be so greedy,*
> *You got so fat, though once you were so spindly.*
> *Your big fat tummy caught the eye of Farmer Jones,*
> *And now you're just a pile of bones.*

133

Of course, the story of Tom Gobble is not just a story about a turkey. It's a story about us, too, because we can also be pretty greedy at times. It seems that we always want to be first in line, to have the best seat or the biggest cookie; and at the dinner table our hands are a blur as we grab for the chicken or the rolls.

The opposite of being grabby or greedy is being thankful. In the Bible we read: "O give thanks to the Lord, for Yahweh* is good; God's steadfast love endures for ever!"

Of course it's easy to be thankful at Thanksgiving time. But wouldn't it be great to be thankful each and every day? I have an idea. Are you willing to give it a try? Before our Thanksgiving dinner, we could ask God to help us be a little more thankful and a little less greedy. And — here is my idea — we could ask this not only on Thanksgiving Day but every day. The first thing we could do when we wake up in the morning is to offer a little prayer: "Dear God, I thank you for this day." It's really just as easy as it sounds — we only have to remember to do it. And I hope the story of Tom Gobble will help us to remember.

Reflection Note: In the story of Tom Gobble, the difference between being greedy and being thankful is a matter of life and death. But isn't it the same in the real world when thousands are dying of starvation every day? This is food for thought if we aim this sermon toward older children and young people.

---

*Yahweh is the vocalization of one of the Hebrew names for God. I use it because it is distinctive and therefore conveys a sense of mystery and awe (as it did originally). It is in keeping with my practice to use inclusive language.

Prophets

These sermons are intended to exemplify the meaning of the term "prophetic" in both biblical and contemporary settings.

A Special Note

Children's ideas about prophets are hazy at best. Most children think of prophets as men who lived a long time ago with the ability to predict future events. Their gift to foresee the future was, and is, predicated upon sizing up the direness of the situation at hand. And though children may have a faint idea about why the prophets were important, they will probably not know what it means to be a prophetic church today.

Prophets were primarily those who took faith out of the temple and into the marketplace of human affairs. Needless to say, prophets, both male and female, did and do more *forth*-telling than *fore*-telling, and children ought to know that Martin Luther King, Jr., is part of the prophetic tradition in a way that Jeane Dixon is not.

Prophets also stood apart because of their double message of judgment *and* hope, so we should avoid depicting them in purely negative terms. When they spoke of God's pending judgment, they always balanced it with positive assurances: "God wants you to be his people: God believes you can be his light unto the nations. But if you persist in your ways ..." (cf. Jeremiah 18:5ff.). The prophets also stressed the corporate — they were concerned about the redemption of the nation — so we must be careful not to individualize or trivialize their message.

I have included this special section on the prophets because I fear the Church is not raising up new prophets who know what it means to stand in the marketplace proclaiming God's message of liberation (judgment and hope). If we fail this generation, the next generation will pay the price.

How Will We Turn Out?

Text: Jeremiah 18:1-11*

Appropriate Day: Independence Day

Summary: God still has great hopes that America will be a shining example to other nations.

Props: Modeling clay and one piece of brittle clay

This morning I have brought with me a lump of modeling clay. If we had the time I would give each of you a lump of it to shape into a pot or a cup. I also wish I had a potter's wheel, because that would make it much easier to form this lump of clay into something useful. This is something most of you have probably seen — a potter shaping a pot as he sits at his turning wheel.

Before we go any further, let me read a passage from the book of Jeremiah that speaks about the art of pottery. (*Read or summarize Jeremiah 18:1-11.*)

When Jeremiah went down to the potter's house, he observed that when a pot made of soft clay turns out wrong, the potter simply throws it back on the wheel and starts again, shaping it until it is right. But if the clay has hardened and set, as this piece has, then the potter can do nothing with it. You see, it just crumbles in my hands. (*Break the brittle clay into pieces.*) It is much easier to work with this lump of clay (*knead fresh clay*) because it is still moist and soft. (*Continue working the clay into a pot. If this seems too difficult to do on the spot, get a good start on it beforehand. You can re-use this pot later in "Breaking Pots."*)

These Bible verses suggest that we might think of America as a lump of soft, unshaped clay. God wants very much for America to be a beautifully shaped and useful pot, and Yahweh will help us become that, if we are willing. If we stop and think about it, we realize we can let God be the potter in many ways. We can treat all people equally, regardless of where they came from, how they look or speak, what color their skin is, or how much money they have. We can be generous when our land grows more food than we need. We can choose leaders who are good examples. And, finally, we can show courage enough to stand beside those nations that are struggling for their freedom and dignity.

Since this is the Sunday before the Fourth of July, which is Independence Day, I've been thinking about the birth of our nation. And I've realized that ever since we won our freedom from England, the eyes of the world have been upon us. This is still very true today: The world watches every move we make to see if we mean what we say, and to see what kind of nation we are. You might say that the word is watching to see how we'll turn out. It's like the time that the prophet Jeremiah went down to the potter's house. This great nation of ours could turn out to be very beautiful, or it could become stubborn and brittle and be cast aside as useless.

---

*The first time I gave this sermon I interpreted the text in a personal manner: the clay was the lives of the children. But when I reread the text I knew I had done the prophet a great injustice, for one of the characteristics of a prophetic ministry is to interpret God's will in terms of nations and their leaders. My exegesis also made me see the thread of hope that runs through these chapters.

Breaking Pots

Text: Jeremiah 19:1-11

Appropriate Day: Independence Day, any Sunday

Summary: A prophet is a person who is not afraid to tell the nation when it has stopped trusting in God.

Props: The clay pot previously made in "How Will We Turn Out?"

This morning I have two things I would like you to look at. The first one is a certain phrase that is inscribed on our coins. If anyone has a penny, nickel, a dime, or a quarter, take it out and see if you can find the words "In God We Trust" on it. You'll have to look hard, because the print is small, but it's there.

Our nation, like the ancient nation of Israel, was formed at a time when its leaders and its people had put their trust in God. And the American people are like the Hebrew people in another important way. We both came into a promised land, a land flowing with milk and honey — in other words, a land that was good enough to give us enough food so that no one would go hungry. The pilgrims came across the ocean and the Hebrews crossed the Jordan River, and both nations began by believing that God could be trusted. And that is why you will find inscribed on our coins the phrase "In God We Trust."

The other thing I brought with me is this pot. Some of you may remember it as the pot I started to make as I was talking about the prophet Jeremiah. It's finished now, as you can see. (*Show to children.*) It has also become hard and brittle, which means that it will break easily. I hope you also remember that Jeremiah wanted the Hebrew nation of Judah to be like soft clay so that God could continue to shape her. But Yahweh was afraid that the people of Judah had become so hard and so brittle that they no longer trusted in God. They began to worship gods they made with their hands

— called graven images — and they began to say to themselves, "We will do whatever we want. We don't need God anymore. We don't need God's commandments, and we don't need God's forgiveness. If we want to depend upon our own strength to fight our enemies, we will do just that."

I would like you to think with me for a moment about this question: Does America still trust in God? Do our leaders, do the people of _____ (*name your city*), do you and I forget God? Do we say to ourselves in so many words, "We will do whatever *we* think is right. We don't need God anymore; we can get along very well without God. We're strong enough to defend ourselves." (*Pause to give the children time to reflect on these questions.*)

Jeremiah believed he knew the answer to these questions for his country of Judah. You might say that he was more than unhappy with the people and their leaders — he was angry!

I want you to keep in mind that a prophet is someone who is not afraid to stand up and speak out when he knows a sacred agreement with God has been broken. This is what a prophet does, regardless of the time in which he lives. Jeremiah spoke and he preached, but no one would listen to his words. And so Jeremiah took a clay pot — a pot like this one that's hard and can no longer be reshaped — and he said to the people of Judah, "Since you will not hear my words, I give you this sign of warning. Either you trust in God or, like this pot, you will be broken into pieces and scattered across the land." (*Break your pot. It might be best to use a hammer.*)

(*Now that you have everyone's attention, don't moralize.*) Breaking an agreement with God is serious business. Have we broken our covenant with God?

Reflection Note: Be alert to the danger of identifying America with Israel. We are a nation of Christians but not necessarily heirs to the Covenant (the Church is, but not the United States). Prophets must speak to the nation as well as to the Church, but not always from the same assumption or claims. Being a nation in which Christians are a majority does not make us a Christian nation. Thus in many cases the prophet will speak the same imperative to nation and Church but not always from the same indicative.

Jim, The Promise-Mender

Text: Hosea 1:2; 2:19-23

Appropriate Day: Any Sunday

Summary: A prophet is someone who makes us remember a promise we made with God.

Props: Handwritten signs bearing the messages mentioned below (Post them as you are telling the story.)

We have all had the experience of making a promise to someone. If it was a very, very important promise, we may remember how it turned out — was the promise remembered and kept, or forgotten and never kept?

Promises we know about; prophets we aren't so sure about. The story I tell you now is of a boy and a promise and how he became a prophet.

Jim was looking forward to the special fishing trip he and his father had talked about several weeks ago. His father had promised they could go on Saturday. Today was only Monday, but Jim was making sure his fishing pole was ready to go — even though his father hadn't said anything more about the trip. When Saturday morning came, Jim got up early and went into his father's bedroom to wake him up. "Dad, it's time to get up," Jim whispered in his ear. "We're going fishing, remember?"

"Fishing trip?" his dad questioned by the tone of his voice. "What fishing trip?"

"The one you promised," answered Jim.

"I don't remember making any promise," his father said.

Jim's heart sank. He went back to his room, and as he sat on the edge of his bed, he could feel his disappointment turning to anger. "How could my father forget?" he asked. If only he could get his father to remember his promise. Then Jim had an idea. He would tape various signs where his father would be sure to see them.

Half an hour later, Jim had posted his signs. On the car the sign read, "Going Fishing"; on the refrigerator door, "Monday, April 21" (*that was the day his father had made the promise*). The sign on his father's desk said, "Bowe Lake." But the biggest sign of all he taped to his father's bedroom door. It read, "Promise-Breaker." But there was no change. The signs came down and his father said nothing.

That night Jim prayed to God. Perhaps that is why the next morning he made a new sign — a sign that covered his father's bedroom door. It read, "I Love You!"

When his father sat down for Sunday breakfast, he called Jim to join him. "Jim," he said with a twinkle in his eyes, "I couldn't help noticing the new sign on my door that says, 'I love you.' I guess it means you aren't angry with me anymore. And I have a confession to make. The fishing trip we missed — I do remember the promise. I had forgotten about it, and then I wasn't Christian enough to admit I had forgotten it. I was a promise-breaker. But you and your sign made me want very much to remember. Can we start again and make a new promise agreement — one that I will be sure to remember?"

My story of Jim the promise-mender is also a story of Jim the prophet, because prophets are like Jim. They get angry when we break the promises we've made with God. Prophets long ago got angry when Israel forgot, or simply didn't care, about the promises she had made with God. But they also told the people of Israel that God still loved them. Prophets today are also like Jim when they remind us about the promises we have made to help the poor and make the world a safe place to live.

And, just like Jim, you can be a prophet in your own way. I know you will speak up when someone you love breaks a promise to you. And please speak up, too, when you believe any of us who are Christians are not keeping our promises to God.

Reflection Note: We usually compare contemporary role models with biblical models ("... because Jim is like an Old Testament prophet"), but in this story I reversed the comparison ("... because Old Testament prophets are like Jim"). Because this story is targeted for younger children, I began it with a contemporary example, which they can understand without an historical framework. I also made a conscious effort, particularly because of the target age, to avoid the sticky business of making prophets the conscience of the nation. (See the Note in "Breaking Pots": America as a nation has not necessarily entered into a covenantal promise with God — at least not by popular vote.)

Puppets

Invite puppets into your chancel. They sing
and dance, fight and make up, play tricks and
tell stories. They are our inner voices and
everyone listens when they speak.

A Special Note

Hand puppets invite their listeners into an imaginary but real world. Since the world of puppets is imaginary, there is a unique freedom to voice a wide range of feelings from anger to envy, disappointment to pride, joy to grief. The truth is this: their imaginary world is the most real world of all for younger children. Puppets introduce situations, solve problems, stir emotions, play tricks, confront, make us laugh, and speak the gospel in a language children understand. If this is a brave new world for you, leap in and soon you'll have puppets multiplying faster than you can name them.

Puppets charm their audience into attention. I do not like to admit it, but children always listen to what my puppets have to say, while often ignoring me. I can't fully explain it and don't have to. When children become the puppeteers, another dynamic happens. Living in a world of giants, they are eager to have the opportunity to manipulate someone smaller than themselves. And as it happens in the hand of an adult, the puppet releases a freedom to voice feelings. As children talk to and for their puppets, they do so openly and honestly.

Puppets create community. As your puppets and the children get to know each other, they will create a new community. My cast of characters evolved over time without much forethought. If you are starting from scratch, you have the opportunity to begin to write down the personality of each puppet with some intention. If you are not consistent in separating the personalities, the children will become confused. As you create your cast of characters, keep in mind the personalities and inner voices of the children of your congregation. Here is my cast:

Oscar the Grouch — He is the instigator, the doubter. It is difficult for Oscar to greet you with a cheerful "hello" because he seems always to have gotten out of bed on the wrong side. Oscar asks the tough questions.

Squeaky the Church Mouse — Often paired with Oscar because she is the cheerful companion you would invite on a trip.

146

Because of her diminutive size, Squeaky has a slight inferiority complex but her faith "wins out" in the end.

Leo the Lion — There is nothing shy or humble about Leo, especially when compared to Squeaky. He is the bully, the superior type. You know when he is coming and you wish he would leave.

Henly the Hedgehog — He comes from England with a stiff upper lip, cares about manners, correct English, and doing things properly. He is always logical and formal but has a heart of gold.

Izzy — He is your off-the-wall nut. Speaks with a Spanish accent (if you can pull it off), is always on the go, a frenetic whirlwind. He is an *A* personality, the ultimate achiever, and always needs to be *the best*. He gives hugs and kisses and is known to bite a nose or two.

Flopsy the Long-eared Rabbit — Because of her long ears, the other creatures often make fun of Flopsy, but she stands her ground with humor. She is soft, kindhearted, gullible, and knows shame and guilt.

My habit is not to write out a script but to practice with the voices beforehand.[15] As the puppets exude their particular personalities, the script will write itself. Without a script, though, give more attention to the clarity of your message.

God Doesn't Make Telephone Calls

Text: Isaiah 55:8

Season: Any

Summary: Talking with God is heart to heart and not like telephoning "the Big guy up there."

Props: Puppets, telephone (wireless would be the best)

Note: While I do not recommend sermons with a negative message, there is a tradition that emphasizes the incomprehensibility of God. We must be careful not to teach those things that will need to be unlearned later, namely, that it is possible to have a direct communication with God.

Flopsy: Ring, ring. (*Turns to the children.*) I'm trying to ring up Leo.

Leo: (*Comes prancing in.*) If you are trying to telephone me, hang up because I'm here. And if you haven't heard — and I can't believe you haven't — *I don't have a telephone.* Don't need one. If you want me, come and find me.

Flopsy: Well, excuse me. I thought everyone had a telephone. Then how can I talk to you?

Leo: Like this. (*Presses his face up against Flopsy's.*) And I suppose you are the kind of person who thinks she can telephone God. (*Goes to the telephone.*) Just as easy as dialing God, yeah?

Flopsy: All right, I have tried to telephone God. I've tried G-O-D A-L-M-I-G-H-T-Y, Y-A-H-W-E-H.

148

Leo: Sometimes you amaze me, Flopsy. I thought everyone knew you can't just "ring up" God. It doesn't work that way.

Flopsy: Why not?

Leo: Because God is God and God doesn't take telephone calls.

Flopsy: Oh.

Leo: The way you talk with God is heart-to-heart. You have to stop talking and listen.

Flopsy: And then you will hear God talking?

Leo: Not exactly. I can't explain it. I know it isn't like picking up the phone and talking to a friend. It's ... it's like wordless. It's hard. It takes practice. It's something too hard to explain.

Flopsy: Talking with God is like the two of us here, face-to-face. Only you can't see the face of God.

Leo: It's as I said: heart-to-heart. Give it a try, Flopsy. I know you can do it.

Jesus Loves Me, This I Know

Text: Matthew 19:13-15

Season: Any

Summary: Jesus loves me, this I know, for the Bible tells me so.

Props: Puppets

Izzy: Oh me, oh my, I don't know what I am going to do!

Henly: What is the matter? You look all out of sorts.

Izzy: Oh me, oh my, I tell you, I don't know what I am going to do. The sky is falling!

Henly: And who told you that?

Izzy: It was the chicken.

Henly: The chicken told you the sky is falling? And you believed the chicken?

Izzy: I do, I do. Oh me, oh my, I don't know what I am going to do!

Henly: Do you believe everything you are told?

Izzy: (*Pauses.*) No, man, of course not.

Henly: Well, look at the sky. (*Izzy looks up.*) Is the sky falling?

Izzy: I don't believe it is.

Henly: Do you believe Jesus loves you?

Izzy: (*Pauses.*) Why should I? I know I can't trust the chicken. I am not sure I can trust you.

Henly: You don't have to trust me. I am telling you Jesus loves you because the Bible says it is so.

Izzy: The Bible says it is so! Wow! (*Pauses.*) And why should I believe the Bible?

Henly: Izzy, the Bible isn't like the chicken who can run around without its head. The Bible was written by many, many men and women who knew how much God loved them. And so they wrote it down along with a lot of stories about God's love.

Izzy: You know what, I'm feeling better. The sky isn't falling and God loves me. Oh me, oh my, I'm feeling just great.

Henly: Glad to hear it.

What Color Is God's Skin?*

Text: Genesis 1:27

Season: Any

Summary: This kind of literal question is best answered with a little playfulness.

Props: Puppets

Squeaky: Good morning to you, Oscar.

Oscar: If you say so, but for myself, I am going to wait and see.

Squeaky: Oscar, can I ask you a question?

Oscar: Won't hurt, I suppose.

Squeaky: What color is God's skin?

Oscar: So early in the morning for such a deep question. Why do you ask?

Squeaky: Because your fur is shaggy brown but mine is mouse grey and Leo's is lion tan and Izzy is Caribbean green.

Oscar: Some people I know are white, some are brown, others yellow and black; though, come to think of it, I have never met a green person.

Squeaky: So, now you see why I ask. Everybody is a different color. So what color is God's skin?

Oscar: And I don't have an answer because I have never seen God. Have you?

Squeaky: Of course not.

Oscar: Maybe God is all the colors of the rainbow.

Squeaky: Maybe God doesn't even have skin.

Oscar: Wouldn't that be a hoot? Everyone thinking that only they are made in the likeness of God and God is no color at all.

Squeaky: Or, God is some color we have never heard of!

Oscar: Wow, that's been some heavy thinking. It must be time for me to go back to bed and if I ever do meet a green person, I will ask, "What color is God's skin?"

---

*This sermon was inspired by "What Color Is God's Skin," words and music by Thomas Wilkes and David Stevenson.

Postscript

Since this book is about creativity as much as it is about theology, I would appreciate hearing from you. We share creativity not so much to copy or reproduce it but to spark the creative spirit within all of us. God's grace and love have touched your life in a different way than they have touched mine. In discussing lifestyles, Henry Thoreau stated it this way:

> I would not have anyone adopt **my** mode of living on any account; for, beside that before he has fairly learned it I may have found out another for myself, I desire that there may be as many different persons in the world as possible; but I would have each one be very careful to find out and pursue **his own** way....

Correspondence — ideas about experiments, successes and failures, sermons, stories, gospel participations, and so forth — may be mailed to this address:

Rev. Richard Coleman
48 Old Cart Path Lane
Pembroke, MA 02359
rcoleman20@earthlink.net

Endnotes

1. In *Children in the Worshipping Community* (John Knox Press, 1981), David Nag and Virginia Thomas argue *against* children's sermons or a special time for children within the worship service and argue *for* an integrated worship service. They are perfectly correct when they say, "Worship can have the depth of content and the integrity that reflect the highest biblical and traditional standards and at the same time have appeal to children" (p. 24). On the other hand, we are presupposing the ideal situation and never grapple with the negative aspects of having children present for the entire worship service or what we are forced to sacrifice (such as a full hour of Christian education). The ideal I have in mind is for children to experience *both* worship that is most excellent and in no way "watered down" and worship that is for children with children participating as leaders. There are various ways to achieve this. See the discussion in Iris V. Cully, *Christian Worship and Church Education* (Philadelphia: Westminster Press, 1967). My overall impression is that most worship leaders ignore the presence of children except for the children's sermon.

2. We must take into account the tendency of the early Church to close off the open-ended quality of Jesus' style of teaching by adding their interpretation or by transposing the parable-story into a new context. See Crossan, *In Parables* (New York: Harper & Row, 1973), and Joachim Jeremias, *The Parables of Jesus* (New York: Charles Scribner's Sons, 1963).

3. The learning pyramid is hypothetical since learning is individual and age dependent, but as a generalization it is true. If the reader wishes to pursue learning theory as it relates to religions development and change, I recommend Thomas Groome, *Christian Education: Sharing Our Story and Vision* (San Francisco: Harper & Row, 1980); Jerome W. Berryman, *Godly Play: A Way of Religious Education* (New York: HarperSanFrancisco, 1991); and James E. Loder, *The Transforming Moment: Understanding Convictional Experiences* (San Francisco: Harper & Row, 1981).

4. For an extended discussion of sermon planning that leads the congregation, see Richard J. Coleman, "What Aggravates Me About the Preaching I Hear," *The Pulpit* (December, 1968).

5. Gabriel Fackre has approached the reading of Scripture in a very practical and dramatic way. See his *The Christian Story: A Narrative Interpretation of Basic Christian Doctrine*, vols. 1, 2 (Grand Rapids: William B. Eerdmans, 1978, 1984, 1987, 1996).

6. While not specifically about child development, James Fowler and Sam Keen's *Life Maps: Conversation on the Journey to Faith* (Waco: Word Books, 1978) remains a very accessible entry into the discussion of religious development.

7. A number of publishers come to mind such as Concordia, Hope, Augsburg. While these publishers primarily offer separate anthems for distinct choirs, there is sufficient flexibility to allow for greater intergenerational participation. An adult anthem, for example, may have a part for "congregational response," and this can be fulfilled by the junior choir. Rotermund's *Children Sing His Praise* has quite a complete listing of resources except for Spectrum Music (1844-B Massachusetts Ave., Lexington, MA).

8. A particular helpful resource is *The Creative Use of Choirs in Worship* by Hal H. Hopson. This handbook of creative arrangements is paired with two other handbooks by Hopson: *The Creative Use of Handbells in Hymn Singing* and *The Creative Use of Instruments in Worship*. They are available through Hope Publishing Company, 380 S. Main Pl., Carol Stream, IL 60187.

9. See Richard A. Jensen, *Telling the Story* (Minneapolis: Augsburg, 1980), and John Shea, *Stories of God* (Chicago: Thomas More Press, 1978). The renaissance of the story form of proclamation is concurrent with reading the Bible as narrative. For the latter see Stanley Hauerwas and L. Gregory Jones, ed., *Why Narrative?* (Grand Rapids: William B. Eerdmans, 1989). Also see note 5.

10. Frederick Buechner's commencement address, "The Two Stories," published by Bangor Theological's *Open Door* (summer 1980).

11. Fred B. Craddock, *Overhearing the Gospel* (Nashville: Abingdon, 1978), p. 118.

12. As both a classic presentation and one of the first scholars to disclose this hermeneutical principle, Gerhard von Rad stands apart. See his *Old Testament Theology*, 2 vols. (New York: Harper & Row, 1962).

13. See Bruno Bettelheim, *The Uses of Enchantment* (New York: Alfred A. Knopf, 1976), p. 25.

14. William J. Bennett, *The Book of Virtues for Young People* (Parsippany, NJ: Simon & Schuster, 1996).

15. A very helpful resource is Joan Sercl's *Puppet Scripts for Sunday Mornings*.

Bibliography

Bennett, William. *The Book of Virtues for Young People: A Treasury of Great Moral Stories*. Parsippany, New Jersey: Simon & Schuster, 1996.

Berryman, Jerome W. *Godly Play: A Way of Religious Education*. New York: HarperSanFrancisco, 1991.

Bettelheim, Bruno. *The Uses of Enchantment*. New York: Alfred A. Knopf, 1976.

Brueggemann, Walter. *David's Truth*. Minneapolis: Fortress, 1985.

_____. *Finally Comes the Poet*. Minneapolis: Fortress, 1989.

Buechner, Frederick. "The Two Stories." In *Open Door*. Bangor: Bangor Theological Seminary (summer 1980).

Carr, Jo, and Imogene Sorley. *Bless This Mess & Other Prayers*. Nashville: Abingdon, 1969.

Coleman, Richard J., "What Aggravates Me About the Preaching I Hear." *The Pulpit* (December, 1968), pp. 22-25.

Craddock, Fred B. *Overhearing the Gospel*. Nashville: Abingdon, 1978.

Crossan, John Dominic. *In Parables*. New York: Harper & Row, 1973.

Cully, Iris V. *Christian Worship and Christian Education*. Philadelphia: Westminster Press, 1967.

Donaldson, Margaret. *Children's Minds*. New York: W. W. Norton & Company, 1978.

Duska, Ronald, and Mariellen Whelan. *Moral Development: A Guide to Piaget and Kohlberg*. New York: Paulist Press, 1975.

Fannin, Kathleen. *Cows In Church: 52 Biblically Based Children's Sermons*. Lima, Ohio: CSS Publishing Co., Inc., 1999.

Fowler, James, and Sam Keen. *Life Maps: Conversations on the Journey to Faith*. Waco: Word Books, 1978.

Groome, Thomas. *Christian Religious Education: Sharing Our Story and Vision*. San Francisco: Harper & Row, 1980.

Hauerwas, Stanley, and L. Gregory Jones. *Why Narrative?* Grand Rapids: William B. Eerdmans, 1989.

Hopson, Hal H. *The Creative Use of Choirs In Worship*. Carol Stream, Illinois: Hope Publishing Co., 1999.

Jensen, Richard A. *Telling the Story*. Minneapolis: Augsburg, 1980.

Jeremias, Joachim. *The Parables of Jesus*. New York: Charles Scribner's Sons, 1963.

Johnson, D. B. *Henry Builds a Cabin*. Boston: Houghton Mifflin, 2002.

Jordan, Jerry Marshall. *The Brown Bag* (series). New York: The Pilgrim Press, 1978, 1980.

Keck, Leander E. *Who Is Jesus?* Columbia: University of South Carolina Press, 2000.

Loder, James E. *The Transforming Moment: Understanding Convictional Experiences*. San Francisco: Harper & Row, 1981.

Nag, David, and Virginia Thomas. *Children in the Worshipping Community*. Atlanta: John Knox Press, 1981.

Quoist, Michael. *Prayers*. New York: Sheed & Ward, 1963.

Rotermund, Donald. *Children Sing His Praise: A Handbook for Children's Choir Directors*. St. Louis: Concordia, 1985.

Satir, Virginia. *People Making*. Palo Alto: Science and Behavior Books, 1972.

Sercl, Joan M. *Puppet Scripts for Sunday Mornings*. Nashville: Abingdon Press, 1996.

Shea, John. *Stories of God: An Unauthorized Biography*. Chicago: Thomas More Press, 1978.

Stewart, Sonja M., and Jerome W. Berryman. *Young Children and Worship*. Louisville: Westminster/John Knox, 1989.

Van de Wetering, Janwillem. *The Empty Mirror*. Boston: Houghton Mifflin, 1974.

Von Rad, Gerhard. *Old Testament Theology*. 2 vols. New York: Harper & Row, 1962.

Westerhoff, John H. *Bringing up Children in the Christian Faith*. Minneapolis: Winston Press, 1980.

_____. *Will Our Children Have Faith?* New York: Seabury Press, 1976.

Wilder, Amos. *Early Christian Rhetoric: The Language of the Gospel*. Cambridge: Harvard University Press, 1971.